新大学英语

总主编 庄智象
系列主编 华先发

听视说教程

4

LISTENING · WATCHING · SPEAKING

教师用书
Teacher's Book

本书主编 于 弋

编 者 吴静怡 华满元
于 弋 余新星
王 冲

华东师范大学出版社
·上海·

图书在版编目（CIP）数据

新大学英语·听视说教程 4 教师用书 / 华先发系列主
编；于戈本书主编. —上海：华东师范大学出版社，
2022

ISBN 978-7-5760-1485-3

Ⅰ. ①新… Ⅱ. ①华… ②于… Ⅲ. ①英语—听说教
学-高等学校-教学参考资料 Ⅳ. ①H319.9

中国版本图书馆CIP数据核字（2022）第120827号

新大学英语·听视说教程 4（教师用书）

总 主 编　庄智象
系列主编　华先发
本书主编　于　戈
策划编辑　王　焰　龚海燕
责任编辑　顾晨溪　陆易蓉
责任校对　曹一凡　时东明
装帧设计　俞　越
项目研发　上海时代教育出版研究中心
项目统筹　王　乐

出版发行　华东师范大学出版社
社　　址　上海市中山北路3663号　邮编 200062
网　　址　www.ecnupress.com.cn
电　　话　021－60821666　行政传真 021－62572105
客服电话　021－62865537　门市（邮购）电话 021－62869887
地　　址　上海市中山北路3663号华东师范大学校内先锋路口
网　　店　http://hdsdcbs.tmall.com

印 刷 者　上海邦达彩色包装印务有限公司
开　　本　889×1194　16开
印　　张　15
字　　数　439千字
版　　次　2022年9月第1版
印　　次　2022年9月第1次
书　　号　ISBN 978－7－5760－1485－3
定　　价　75.00元

出 版 人　王　焰

"新大学英语"系列教材编委会

顾　问：胡文仲　杨惠中　戴炜栋　秦秀白

编　委：（按姓氏拼音排序）

曹　进（西北师范大学）	马　萧（武汉大学）
常　辉（上海交通大学）	马金芳（青海师范大学）
陈　菁（厦门大学）	潘　红（福州大学）
陈宏俊（大连理工大学）	潘海英（吉林大学）
陈向京（西安交通大学）	彭　静（重庆大学）
陈新仁（南京大学）	强巴央金（西藏大学）
程　工（浙江大学）	束定芳（上海外国语大学）
程朝翔（石河子大学）	孙勇彬（南京财经大学）
董洪川（四川外国语大学）	屠国元（宁波大学）
段　峰（四川大学）	王　卓（山东师范大学）
方文开（江南大学）	王传经（国防科技大学）
傅　利（哈尔滨工业大学）	王东风（中山大学）
高　瑛（东北师范大学）	王海啸（南京大学）
洪　岗（浙江外国语学院）	王俊菊（山东大学）
胡　强（湘潭大学）	王守仁（南京大学）
胡美馨（浙江师范大学）	卫乃兴（北京航空航天大学）
黄国文（华南农业大学）	吴　赟（同济大学）
季佩英（复旦大学）	向明友（对外经济贸易大学）
姜亚军（西安外国语大学）	肖艳玲（海南大学）
李　颖（杭州师范大学）	谢世坚（广西师范大学）
李清平（中南大学）	杨朝军（河南大学）
李淑静（北京大学）	杨连瑞（中国海洋大学）
李霄翔（东南大学）	叶慧君（河北大学）
李勇忠（江西师范大学）	原一川（云南师范大学）
李正栓（河北师范大学）	张　红（内蒙古工业大学）
梁晓冬（河南师范大学）	张树德（广西科技大学）
刘　瑾（贵州师范大学）	张文霞（清华大学）
刘　芹（上海理工大学）	张耀平（山西大学）
刘承宇（西南大学）	赵　雯（暨南大学）
刘建达（广东外语外贸大学）	钟书能（华南理工大学）
刘建喜（天津外国语大学）	周玉忠（宁夏大学）
刘正光（湖南大学）	朱　跃（安徽大学）
罗良功（华中师范大学）	朱晓映（华东师范大学）

总 序
Foreword

　　处在经济全球化、政治多极化、科技一体化、信息网络化、文化多元化的浪潮中，以及世界百年未有之大变局的形势下，无论是追求和平发展，文化交融、文明互鉴，构建人类命运共同体，还是面对新形势、新任务、新要求，迎接新机遇、新挑战，都需要我国的高等教育能够培养出更多的既有家国情怀，又有国际视野，能够参与国际合作和竞争的高素质的专业人才。高质量的教材无疑不可或缺。为此我们组织、策划编写了"新大学英语"系列教材。

　　"新大学英语"系列教材是贯彻教育部《大学英语课程教学要求》和《大学英语教学指南》等文件精神，准确把握教学目标、要求和任务，并在对上百所高校大学英语教学状况调查分析和未来发展趋势及需求研判的基础上研发、编写而成。既适宜当下的教学需求，又有一定的前瞻性。

　　"新大学英语"系列教材由《综合教程》、《听视说教程》、《跨文化交际阅读教程》和《写作教程》的学生用书和教师用书（各1至4册）构成，可以充分满足大学英语教学需要，完成教学任务，达到教学要求，实现教学目标。为新时代掌握外语、精通专业，具有家国情怀，通晓国际规则，能够参与国际合作和竞争的创新型专业人才奠定扎实的英语知识和英语综合运用能力基础。

　　"新大学英语"系列教材主要特色是：

1. 落实立德树人的根本任务

　　"新大学英语"系列教材在编写中努力将全面贯彻党的教育方针、落实立德树人的根本任务贯穿于英语知识学习、文化认知和英语能力培养的全过程。坚持正确导向，从课文选择与编写，练习设计与撰写，问题设置与讨论等各个方面，努力传导正能量，引导和激励学生积极进取，奋发向上，引导学生坚定"四个自信"，践行社会主义核心价值观，树立正确的世界观、人生观和价值观，努力成为既有家国情怀，又有国际胸怀的中国特色社会主义建设者和接班人。

2. 坚持工具性和人文性的统一

大学英语课程是一门语言基础课程，是高校人文教育的一个重要组成部分，兼有工具性和人文性双重性质。工具性体现在学生应达到的听、说、读、写、译的能力方面，主要通过语言知识、文化知识的学习和技能的训练获得；人文性体现在以人为本，人文情怀，弘扬科学精神，注重人的综合素质培养和关注人的全面发展方面，主要通过文化知识学习，情感培养和人文精神熏陶而造就。语言学习的工具性和人文性是不可分割的，工具性中体现人文性，人文性中兼有工具性。二者互为依存，互为包容，互为促进。

3. 准确定位、满足教学需要

根据《大学英语课程教学要求》和《大学英语教学指南》等文件要求，参考对高中和大学英语现状的调查分析，"新大学英语"系列教材将教学目标定为基础、提高和发展三个层次或阶段，就各个阶段的英语综合应用能力和听、说、读、写、译专项技能给出描述。第一、二册按基础目标要求编写，第三、四册按提高和发展目标要求编写。整套教材在英语知识传授、文化学习、语言技能训练和综合能力及素质的培养等方面，遵循分级分类、循序渐进原则，体现和满足教学文件规定的大学英语教学基础目标、提高目标和发展目标的各项要求。

4. 建构合理，可有效完成教学目标

"新大学英语"系列教材依据教学文件提出的要求，着力培养和提升学生听、说、读、写、译综合运用语言能力和跨文化交际意识和能力，编写了《综合教程》、《听视说教程》、《跨文化交际阅读教程》和《写作教程》。各教程分工明确、任务清晰、功能定位准确，既自成体系，又相互照应，可以满足英语知识和文化的学习，语言技能的训练和综合语言运用能力的培养和提升，帮助学生打好语言、知识、文化基本功，培育和提升语言、文化的综合能力和素养，可有效完成教学目标。

5. 内容丰富，形式贴切，练习多样实用，可达到理想的教学要求

"新大学英语"系列教材按主题设计单元、按立德树人标准选择课文、依语言学习规律编写练习。整个系列题材丰富，体裁多样，内容贴近时代、贴近社会、贴近生活，考量当下，瞻望未来。语篇既有宏大叙事，又有微观描述；既探讨社会热点，又讨论学习问题；既围绕大学生学习、生活、情感，又联系社会、国家、未来发展、人类关注；既介绍西方

社会、文化，又注重讲好东方故事，实现文化交融，文明互鉴。各教程内容、主题有机结合，横向纵向相互配合、补充。练习形式多样、实用，生动有趣。内容、主题、练习形成有机统一整体，可达到理想的教学要求。

6. 助力教有实效，学有成效，达到有效学习之目的

"新大学英语"系列教材在单元设计、课文编排、练习设置诸方面，充分考虑中国学生学习英语的环境、认知过程和特点；充分考虑教学需要与特点，以学习者为中心，注重课堂教学环节的科学设计，合理安排每堂课的教学内容和素材。注重传授语言知识、文化知识，通过听、说、读、写、译的单项或综合操练，发展语言技能，培养语感，提升语言综合运用能力，培养正确的学习方法，培育和提升学习能力；注重激发学生学习兴趣和动力，处理好语言输入和输出的关系，帮助学生解决学习中碰到的困难和问题，掌握学习策略等。达到教有实效，学有成效之目的。

7. 继承发展，勇于创新，特色鲜明

"新大学英语"系列教材力求在编写理念、指导思想、编写原则和教学方法等方面既继承和发扬汉语为母语背景下中国学习者学习英语的成功经验和优势，又克服和避免存在的困难和不足，扬长避短，彰显时代特色。从教材的整体框架设计、教程类别的取舍、内容的选择和呈现、练习的设计和编排、教学环节的设置和实施等方面都试图有所创新，以适合当下和未来一个时期的教学需要。如：

1）架构的独特性和新颖性。本系列教材既保留了对学生打好语言基础至关重要的《综合教程》和《听视说教程》，又编有《跨文化交际阅读教程》和《写作教程》，以满足日益频繁的国际交流和交往，以及新媒体、新媒介快速发展对跨文化交际意识培养和写作要求之需。

2）知识和能力的统一。本系列教材注重语言知识和文化知识的传授，力图使知识内化成能力；坚持知识的获取和积累服务于能力的发展，通过大量的语言技能的操练，培育语感，提升语言能力，坚守"没有语言知识，难有语言能力；有了语言知识，未必自然形成语言能力"的观点。努力将二者有机统一起来，促进语言能力发展。

3）《跨文化交际阅读教程》创新性地尝试，将跨文化交际知识学习、意识增强、技能和能力发展融入到阅读篇章、练习的编写之中。通过文本阅读、案例分析与中西文化的讨论和比较等环节培养学习者多元文化意识，增强文化自信，使学习者顺畅进行国际交流与沟通，服务于人类命运共同体的建设。

4）《写作教程》依据语言学习与习得的规律和特点，从架构上作了新的尝试，分别编有"语词与写作"、"语法与写作"、"语篇与写作"和"实用写作"，遵循读写结合、学用结合、思练结合的原则，通过观察、例释、操练和夯实等环节，以逐渐递进的思路和方式，训练和发展学生的写作能力。

8. 配套资源丰富

"新大学英语"系列教材配有网络课件和电子教案，建有网络教学平台和教学资源库，可以有效实现课堂教学和课外自主学习，线下线上教学互动，相互促进，相得益彰。

"新大学英语"系列教材的问世，是编写团队历经数年的学习、探索、实践、研讨，通力合作和辛勤劳动的成果，是智慧和汗水的结晶。各位主编和编者为此牺牲了很多个人的兴趣和爱好，付出了很多辛劳。在此，向他们表示衷心的感谢。祁寿华教授对系列教材进行了认真仔细的审校，谨向他致以诚挚的谢意！华东师范大学出版社的领导对教材编写和出版给予了很多的支持，编辑团队精心编审和设计，保证了教材的出版质量和按时出版发行，谨在此一并致谢。

限于水平和时间，教材难免存在不尽如人意的地方，差错恐难免，恳请老师和同学们提出批评和建议，以期不断完善。

庄智象

2020 年春

编者的话
Editor's Note

《新大学英语·听视说教程》的教师用书共四册，与学生用书四册相配套，采用混合编排的方式编写，内容包括学生用书的全部内容、各单元教学建议、音视频文本、练习参考及答案等。为了帮助教师更好地理解和贯彻本教程的编写理念，精准开展课堂教学，编者就《新大学英语·听视说教程》的编写理念和教学活动作出以下几点说明：

一、编写原则

● 通过听、视、说的有效结合，使学生将所学语言输入充分内化，转化为输出能力；

● 通过模仿和创新，提升学生的实际交流能力；

● 通过分析和综合，增强学生解决问题的能力；

● 通过师生互动和生生互动，提高学生合作学习的能力。

二、教材主题选择与整体设计

主题选择：紧扣大学校园生活实际，各单元主题内容关注学生德、智、体等的全面发展；体裁多为各种相关语境下的对话、访谈、报道和独白。

结构编排：学生用书第一册和第二册的语言输入的顺序设计为"听"在前，"视"在后，旨在夯实大一学生听视说的基础；第三册和第四册将"视"置于"听"之前，旨在聚焦大二学生听视说能力的提升。本册各单元围绕主题组织素材，均通过5个板块展开内容：导入（Warming Up）、视说（Watching and Speaking）、听说（Listening and Speaking）、巩固（Consolidating）、自检（Goal Checking）。本册单元各板块以学习目标为导向；提供本板块出现的新词和相关注解，便于学生课前预习；听力技巧设置于视说板块后，帮助学生掌握相关听力技能；交际技巧设置于听说板块后，并与巩固板块衔接，以巩固和扩展前面课堂所学。

教学设计：依据目前大学英语教学课时数设计。（1）学生用书导入板块要求学生在课前完成，教师可根据具体情况适时检查；（2）视说板块设计2个任务，每个任务配置（A、B）2个练习，教师可根据本校实际情况在课堂上完成全部或A部分的练习；（3）听说板块设计4个任务，教师可根据本校实际情况在课堂上完成全部或前两个任务；（4）巩固板块和自检板块一般安排学生在课后完成。如有的学校课时安排较充裕，可考虑将巩固板块纳入课堂教学范围。

语速控制：由慢速逐步过渡到正常语速。第一册音频和视频的语速为每分钟120—130词；第二册音频和视频的语速为每分钟130—140词；第三册音频和视频的语速为每分钟140—150词；第四册音频和视频的语速为每分钟150—160词。

三、教学设计

教学目标：听力按大学英语等级考试相应等级（三级、四级和六级）的要求来设计，旨在让学生学完后达到相应的听力水平，即能听懂不同场合中一般性话题的语言材料，把握主旨，抓住重点，明晰事实、观点与细节，领悟他人的意图和态度；口头表达亦按大学英语等级考试相应等级（三级、四级和六级）的要求来设计，旨在让学生学完后达到相应的口头表达水平，即能在较为熟悉的场合就学习、工作等话题进行交流、讨论、协商，表明观点和态度，就一般性话题进行有效的描述、说明或阐述，表达准确、连贯、得体，同时体现出良好的分析、综合及评价的思维能力。

教学原则：以建构主义理论为导向，以支架式教学和情景教学为支撑，同时融入思维导图等方法，将合作学习、个性化学习、师生互动、生生互动贯彻始终。本套教材通过单元主题设计、板块设计、练习设计将此教学原则融入其中。

教学模式：根据混合式课堂教学模式进行设计，各册教学内容分别对应《大学英语教学指南（2020）》的要求，遵循教育目标层次理论的分类（识记knowledge、理解comprehension、运用application、分析analysis、综合synthesis和评价evaluation），逐级设计听视说活动，将课前（导入和生词预习，旨在识记，激发学生对本单元主题的学习兴趣）、课中（听说和视说，旨在理解和运用，聚焦学生对听视内容的掌握和口头模仿）和课后（巩固和自测，旨在分析、综合和评价，关注学生对所学内容的灵活运用和学习效果自测）相结合，做到线上和线下相结合。

教学时间分配：各板块教学时间分配建议为Listening and Speaking—40分钟；Watching and Speaking—40分钟；Consolidating—5分钟。教师可根据学校教学实际情况做出适当调整。

Unit 1

Warming Up: Think and Discuss What Makes People Influential

Before you start this unit, finish the following exercises with a partner.

1. Listen to the news and discuss with a partner the accomplishment of the Nobel Prize winner Tu Youyou.

Keys

Using traditional Chinese remedy, Tu Youyou discovered an entirely new anti-malarial treatment, artemisinin, which made possible the treatment of thousands of patients in China in the 1980s.

2. Who is your favorite scientist or celebrity? Discuss with your partner what makes a person influential.

Words and Expressions

parasitic *adj.* living on another animal or plant and getting its food from it 寄生的

physiology *n.* the scientific study of the normal functions of living things 生理学

malarial *adj.* of or infected by malaria which is an infectious disease 疟疾的

artemisinin *n.* a drug obtained from the plant genus Artemisia and used to treat malaria 青蒿素

4

Scripts

The Chinese Nobel Prize winner Tu Youyou has been awarded the UNESCO-Equatorial Guinea International Prize for Research in the Life Sciences for her research into parasitic diseases.

As the winner of the 2015 Nobel Prize in Physiology or Medicine, Professor Tu Youyou of the China Academy of Chinese Medical Sciences discovered an entirely new anti-malarial treatment, artemisinin, which made possible the treatment of thousands of patients in China in the 1980s.

Speaking at the awarding ceremony at the AU Headquarters in Addis Ababa, Audrey Azoulay, Director-General of UNESCO has paid tribute to Tu Youyou for her contributions to humanity.

"Her work is revolutionary; she used traditional Chinese remedy in order to provide a new treatment for malaria," the Director-General noted. "She is among the ones who have received the Nobel Prize; she has used indigenous knowledge, and we are very proud in UNESCO because we have a specific program which is very ambitious to develop the position of women in sciences."

Watching and Speaking: Influential People in the World

▶ Watching

> **Teaching Tips**
>
> 1. Familiarize students with the purpose of this section—identifying influential people and their accomplishments.
> 2. Call students' attention to Words and Expressions, and Notes before watching.
> 3. Have students pay attention to the situation of each task.
> 4. Have students do the tasks and check the answers.

Task 1 A Watch the video clip and choose the best answer to each question you hear.

Situation: Here is a seminar on the most influential people in history.

(D) 1. Which discipline do Aristotle's writings NOT cover?
A. Logic.
B. Aesthetics.
C. Biology.
D. Anthropology.

(A) 2. When was Hawking's black hole theory proposed?
A. In 1971.
B. In 1876.
C. In 1970.
D. In 1771.

(C) 3. What's the use of the black hole area theory?
A. It has helped shape centuries of philosophy.
B. It has helped span a wide range of disciplines.
C. It has helped prove the idea of a "Big Bang".
D. It has helped broaden the evolutionary theory.

Words and Expressions

gauge *v.* to judge 判断

metaphysics *n.* a branch of philosophy dealing with the nature of existence, truth and knowledge 形而上学

aesthetics *n.* a branch of philosophy dealing with beauty and taste 美学

organism *n.* a living thing that has the ability to act or function independently 生物体

inanimate *adj.* not endowed with life 无生命的

Notes

the Renaissance the revival of European art and literature in the 14th–16th centuries under the influence of classical models 文艺复兴时期

general relativity a theory proposed by Einstein in 1916 to deal with gravitation 广义相对论（由爱因斯坦于1916年提出，该理论探讨万有引力）

quantum mechanics a branch of physics which studies the law of moving micro particles 量子力学

Task ② Listen to the passage and choose the best answer to each question you hear.

Situation: Steve Jobs was giving a speech at Stanford University, talking about how he got fired by Apple and then returned to Apple.

(C) **1.** Where did Steve Jobs start the Apple company when he was 20?
A. In his friend's house.
B. In his friend's garage.
C. In his parents' garage.
D. In his parents' garden.

(B) **2.** Why was Jobs fired by the Apple company?
A. Because he used the money of the company in an unlawful way.
B. Because his vision and his teammate's vision were different.
C. Because he hired someone talented to run the company with him.
D. Because he wanted to start another company with his wife.

(B) **3.** Why did Jobs return to Apple?
A. Because Pixar was bought by Apple.
B. Because NeXT was bought by Apple.
C. Because Pixar created a successful studio.
D. Because NeXT was at the heart of Apple.

Words and Expressions

diverge *v.* to differ 分歧
baton *n.* a short stick that is passed from one runner to another in a relay race 接力棒

It's not my work
It's my passion

Scripts

My second story is about love and loss. I was lucky I found what I loved to do early in life. Woz and I started Apple in my parents' garage when I was 20. We worked hard, and in 10 years, Apple had grown from just the two of us in a garage into a $2 billion company with over 4,000 employees. And then I got fired. How can you get fired from a company you started?

As Apple grew, we hired someone I thought was very talented to run the company with me, and things went well for the first year or so. But then our visions of the future began to diverge, and eventually, we had a falling out. So at 30, I was out, and very publicly out. What had been the focus of my entire adult life was gone, and it was devastating. I really didn't know what to do for a few months. I felt that I had let the previous generation of entrepreneurs down—that I had dropped the baton as it was being passed to me. But something slowly began to dawn on me. I still loved what I did. I had been rejected, but I was still in love. And so I decided to start over, and it turned out that getting fired from Apple was the best thing that could have ever happened to me. It freed me to enter one of the most creative periods of my life.

During the next five years, I started a company named NeXT, another company named Pixar. Pixar created the world's first computer-animated feature film, *Toy Story*, and is now the most successful animation studio in the world. In a remarkable turn of events, Apple bought NeXT, I returned to Apple, and the technology we developed at NeXT is at the heart of Apple's current renaissance. Sometimes life hits you in the head with a brick. Don't lose faith. I'm convinced that the only thing that kept me going was that I loved what I did.

Questions

1. Where did Steve Jobs start the Apple company when he was 20?
2. Why was Jobs fired by the Apple company?
3. Why did Jobs return to Apple?

Task 3 Listen to the passage and fill in the blanks with proper expressions.

Situation: Here is a story about the Chinese grassroots Party worker, Huang Wenxiu.

The 30-year-old Party chief of Baini Village in Baise's Leye County had been leading the local (1) poverty-relief work. Her death at such a young age drew huge attention among the locals and netizens on social media, who mourned her death because she had (2) selflessly devoted her life to the well-being of others.

In 2016, Huang graduated from Beijing Normal University with a (3) master's degree. Instead of seeking a career in the capital city, she decided to (4) return to her hometown Baise and was employed by the municipal publicity department.

Hao Haiyan, her university teacher, said that Huang had good English skills, and it wouldn't have been difficult for her to stay in Beijing or (5) go abroad if she'd wanted. Huang, however, believed that her life's work was in helping develop her hometown and (6) bringing hope to more people.

When Huang was appointed Party chief in March 2018, (7) about 23% of the village's 472 families lived in poverty. In 2019, the figure was 2.71%. The area also has four new reservoirs and 17 street lamps.

Huang invited experts to (8) come and show the villagers how to improve production and quality, and reached out to customers online and offline to (9) boost sales of what the village produces. During her stint as Party chief, the area growing oranges increased from 33 hectares to 133 hectares. The income of families growing oranges increased by (10) 2,500 yuan annually on average.

Words and Expressions

flash *adj.* moving or passing very quickly 快速的

netizen *n.* a user of the Internet, esp. a habitual or keen one 网民

municipal *adj.* relating to a town or district or its governing body 市政的

reservoir *n.* a large natural or artificial lake used as a source of water supply 水库

stint *n.* a person's fixed or allotted period of work 任期

Huang Wenxiu didn't know the rainy night in the mountains surrounding the Guangxi Zhuang Autonomous Region's Baise City would be her last. She instead expected it'd be a homecoming to the village where she began her career after graduation.

Huang released a video on social media around midnight of June 16, 2019 that showed lightning and thunder, and roads covered in water. Some of her colleagues were very concerned and told her, "Watch out! Be careful!" Some asked her to quit the trip and stay in a safe place. After 1 a.m., they lost contact with Huang, whose body was later found in a car washed into a valley by the flash flood.

The 30-year-old Party chief of Baini Village in Baise's Leye County had been leading the local poverty-relief work. Her death at such a young age drew huge attention among the locals and netizens on social media, who mourned her death because she had selflessly devoted her life to the well-being of others.

That night, her father, Huang Zhongjie, who was recovering from a liver-cancer surgery, noticed the bad weather and tried to persuade her to stay until the next morning. But she told him, "That's why I have to go now. The village could be flooded tonight."

In 2016, Huang graduated from Beijing Normal University with a master's degree. Instead of seeking a career in the capital city, she decided to return to her hometown Baise and was employed by the municipal publicity department.

Hao Haiyan, her university teacher, said that Huang had good English skills, and it wouldn't have been difficult for her to stay in Beijing or go abroad if she'd wanted. Huang, however, believed that her life's work was helping develop her hometown and bringing hope to more people.

When Huang was appointed Party chief in March 2018, about 23% of the village's 472 families lived in poverty. In 2019, the figure was 2.71%. The area also has four new reservoirs and 17 street lamps.

Huang invited experts to come and show the villagers how to improve production and quality, and reached out to customers online and offline to boost sales of what the village produces. During her stint as Party chief, the area growing oranges increased from 33 hectares to 133 hectares. The income of families growing oranges increased by 2,500 yuan annually on average. One can only imagine what Huang could accomplish in the years and decades ahead if her life had not been cut short at this young age.

Task 4 Listen to the passage and answer the following questions.

Situation: Here is a talk about makings of influential people.

Question 1 Why are influential people not afraid of taking risks or making decisions?

Influential people don't allow themselves to become stuck or paralyzed by an unforeseen situation. They take action, move forward and find a way around roadblocks. They think before they speak, but they don't hesitate to jump in when necessary.

Question 2 Do influential people acknowledge and recognize people around them? How?

Yes, they do. They let others shine, knowing that the success of others doesn't diminish their own achievements. They value those who have been part of their journeys.

Question 3 What are the six virtues of influential people mentioned by the speaker? Briefly summarize them.

Influential people speak thoughtfully and listen. Influential people aren't afraid of taking risks or making decisions. Influential people are constantly learning and growing. Influential people don't allow themselves to become embroiled in trivial matters or silly competitions. Influential people convey optimism. Influential people understand the importance of acknowledging and recognizing those around them.

Words and Expressions

intimidation *n.* the action of threatening someone 恐吓
coercion *n.* pressure 强迫
trait *n.* a distinguishing quality or characteristic of a person 特质
paralyze *v.* to cause to be unable to move all or part of the body 使⋯⋯麻痹
embroil *v.* to get involved in 卷入
trivial *adj.* unimportant 微不足道的

Scripts

Influence can't be achieved through intimidation or coercion. It comes from a person's ability to inspire and motivate those around them. Do you have what it takes to inspire and influence others? Check out these traits to see if you have what sets influential people apart from the rest.

Influential people speak thoughtfully and listen. They mean what they say. Influential people don't engage in gossip or unfounded attacks on other people. They seek to rise above the petty. They create clear and concise messages and effectively communicate their ideas.

Influential people aren't afraid of taking risks or making decisions. They don't allow themselves to become stuck or paralyzed by an unforeseen situation. They take action, move forward and find a way around roadblocks. They think before they speak, but they don't hesitate to jump in when necessary.

Influential people are constantly learning and growing. They understand the importance of cultivating a mind that is open to new ideas and perspectives. They consider themselves students of life, continually upgrading their skills and challenging themselves to expand their knowledge.

Influential people don't allow themselves to become embroiled in trivial matters or silly competitions. They aren't trying to win every argument or steer every conversation. They're looking to truly understand others and help others feel part of something larger than themselves.

Influential people convey optimism. They see possibilities and opportunities that others miss. They inspire us because we want to be like them. They raise us up and make us want to do the right thing, to be the best that we can be, and to keep pushing boundaries.

Influential people understand the importance of acknowledging and recognizing those around them. They let others shine, knowing that the success of others doesn't diminish their own achievements. They value those who have been part of their journeys.

Speaking

Task 1 What have you learned from the stories of the three influential people told in the Listening Section? Work in groups and discuss who you like the best, using some of the expressions listed below in your conversations.

Which of the three influential people do you like best and why?	Of the three people, I like ... best, because ... Among the three people, ... is the most admirable, because ... From my perspective, ... is the most impressive one, because ...
Can you retell the story of the person you selected?	In ..., he/she started his/her career as ... Influenced by ..., he/she decided to ... He/She was devoted to ...
What traits have you learned from the person you selected?	I was moved by his/her ... From ...'s experience, I have learned that ... Inspired by ..., I became aware that ...

Task 2 Prepare a two-minute talk about makings that are indispensable to one's successful career. You may have a discussion with your classmates first and then formulate the talk.

Albert Einstein

Charles Robert Darwin

Zhang Heng

Cai Lun

▶ Communication Skills

Learn to Talk About Influential People

There are various ways to talk about influential people. One of them may include the following steps:

1. **Begin with the introduction of the influential people.**

   - He/She is ...
   - The Nobel Prize winner ...
   - Known/Recognized as ..., he/she ...
   - Do you know ...?
   - The influential people I know are ...

2. **Describe the life experience of the influential people.**

   - He/She was born in ... in ...
   - He/She studied in... and got his/her ...
   - He/She graduated from ...
   - In ..., he/she worked at/was employed by ...
   - He/She was (appointed) ...

3. **Specify the accomplishments of the influential people.**

   - He/She proposed/excelled at ...
   - His/Her writings/discoveries shaped/spanned a wide range of ...
   - His/Her most significant contribution to ... is ...
   - Their achievements help ...
   - He/She was given ... in recognition of his/her ...

4. **Comment on the influential people.**

   - His/Her work is ...
   - Their contributions to ... are ...
   - He/She devoted his/her life to ...
   - Influential people are/convey/understand/speak ...
   - Influential people don't allow themselves to ...

Unit 2

Warming Up: Think and Discuss China's Space Exploration

Before you start this unit, finish the following exercises with a partner.

1. Listen to the news and discuss with a partner how China will build a prototype scientific research station on the moon by 2030.

Keys

China will carry out lunar resource exploration, scientific research and technological experiments in the Chang'e-6, Chang'e-7 and Chang'e-8 missions.

2. What progress has China made in space exploration? Do some research and share what you have found with your partner.

Words and Expressions

lunar *adj.* connected with the moon 月球的

solicit *v.* to try to get sth. 募集

payload *n.* the amount or weight of things or people that a vehicle can carry 有效载荷

prototype *n.* the first design of sth. from which other forms are copied or developed 原型

Scripts

China aims to launch the Chang'e-6 lunar probe to collect samples in the South Pole-Aitken Basin on the far side of the moon around 2024, said a space expert on Saturday. Hu Hao, chief designer of the third stage of China's lunar exploration program, told the China Space Conference, held in Nanjing, that detailed designing on the mission is in progress.

China launched the Chang'e-5 lunar probe in 2020, successfully bringing home 1,731 grams of moon samples. As the followup of the Chang'e-5 mission, the Chang'e-6 mission would also collect lunar samples automatically for comprehensive analysis and research. The China National Space Administration has invited scientists worldwide to participate in the program, offering to carry solicited payloads.

China will carry out lunar resource exploration, scientific research and technological experiments in the Chang'e-6, Chang'e-7 and Chang'e-8 missions, aiming to build a prototype scientific research station on the moon by 2030, Hu added.

Watching and Speaking: Significance of Space Exploration

▶ Watching

> **Teaching Tips**
>
> 1. Familiarize students with the purpose of this section—identifying China's progress in space exploration and understanding the significance of space exploration.
> 2. Call students' attention to Words and Expressions, and Notes before watching.
> 3. Have students pay attention to the situation of each task.
> 4. Have students do the tasks and check the answers.

Task 1 A Watch the video clip and choose the best answer to each question you hear.

Situation: Here is an interview about China's progress in space exploration.

(A) 1. What does Professor Francis think of China's space exploration in the past years?

A. It's been very impressive.   B. It's developing too fast.

C. It's very hard to leapfrog.   D. It's made a big leap.

(D) 2. Which is NOT the significance of the successful launch of the crewed spacecraft Shenzhou-12?

A. It's important in inspiring young people.

B. It paves the way for future space missions.

C. It's useful for future moon or Mars missions.

D. It helps send more people into the space station.

(A) 3. According to Professor Francis, which is the most difficult thing in spaceflight?

A. Mars rover landing.   B. Moon mission.

C. Moon landing.   D. Space cooperation.

Words and Expressions

leapfrog *v.* to progress by large jumps instead of small increases 赶超；跨越

spacecraft *n.* a vehicle that can travel in space 宇宙飞船

afield *adv.* in places or areas that are not near 在远方

rover *n.* a vehicle for exploring the surface of another planet 探测器

Scripts

Reporter: Professor Francis! What do you think of China's space exploration in the past years?

Professor Francis: I should say the development of China's space exploration in the past years has been very impressive. China has been catching up very fast and may be able to leapfrog in some ways.

Reporter: We know China launched the crewed spacecraft Shenzhou-12 on Thursday. What do you think is the potential significance of this successful launch?

Professor Francis: The move on the one hand is important in inspiring the young people and on the other hand, it has paved the way for future space missions. Sending the astronauts to the space station would allow China to start exploring basically the medicine of space and other technology needed to keep people alive in a small metal box in space to better understand the effects on the health of the astronauts.

Reporter: It's important to have further explorations.

Professor Francis: Right! It'll be useful for future moon missions or Mars missions or further afield. You need to understand how they can survive in zero gravity. You need to work on the technology of how you keep them alive, keep the air, the water and food clean.

Reporter: What do you think of China's landing of the Mars rover earlier this year?

Professor Francis: It is perhaps the most difficult thing in spaceflight. For China, to be able to do it successfully on a first try is very impressive.

Reporter: China will continue to engage in international cooperation and exchanges at wider scope and deeper level, and make Chinese space station a space lab that can deliver benefits to mankind. What's your comment on international cooperation in this aspect?

Professor Francis: Space can be a field for more collaboration between foreign countries and China. The technology to make rockets and keep people alive is the same for everybody. I personally have had collaborations with Chinese scientists in this aspect and they are quite necessary.

Reporter: Thanks for your time!

Professor Francis: Thanks for having me.

Questions

1. What does Professor Francis think of China's space exploration in the past years?

2. Which is NOT the significance of the successful launch of the crewed spacecraft Shenzhou-12?

3. According to Professor Francis, which is the most difficult thing in spaceflight?

Task 1 B Watch the video clip again and answer the following questions.

Question 1 What technology will the program of sending the astronauts to the space station allow China to explore?

The medicine of space and other technology needed to keep people alive in a small metal box in space to better understand the effects on the health of the astronauts.

Question 2 What does Professor Francis think of China's landing of the Mars rover?

The landing of the Mars rover is perhaps the most difficult thing in spaceflight. For China, to be able to do it successfully on a first try is very impressive.

Question 3 What are Professor Francis' comments on the collaboration between China and other countries regarding space exploration?

Space can be a field for more collaboration between foreign countries and China. The technology to make rockets and keep people alive is the same for everybody.

Task 2 A Watch the video clip and fill in the blanks with the information you get.

Situation: Here is an introduction of the significance of space exploration.

What lies beyond the earth isn't something all that new. From the dawn of civilization, humans have always been interested in space. We know that (1) ancient Egyptian priests used the position of the sun to predict flooding and built temples that strategically allowed light in during certain parts of the year, and the Mayans aligned their cities to (2) coincide with astronomical events. Exploration isn't just about curiosity. Exploration is necessary for advancement, whether that be for oneself or species. Because humans (3) have explored, we have expanded our scientific knowledge. And because we have expanded our knowledge, our (4) civilizations advance.

Despite mainly being empty, our (5) <u>exploration of space</u> has provided us with an abundance of information. Over just the last few decades, we've determined the approximate age of the universe. We found water on Mars. In 1992, we detected the first exoplanets. Between the years of (6) <u>2004 and 2005</u>, we discovered three new dwarf planets in our solar system. In 2014, we discovered that Enceladus, one of Saturn's moons, was hiding an underwater ocean. There are several examples of this, but I think you (7) <u>get the point</u>.

While these bits of information are interesting, the data can be used to (8) <u>study the universe</u>, further, the machines we built and the methods we use to gather this information provide us with a more direct reward—technology, due to the (9) <u>specialized tools</u> needed to explore space. Some prominent examples of this include camera phones, wireless headsets, memory foam computer mice and even laptops. Many of these examples have become items we use on a daily basis. You may even be using some of them right now. With the help of these (10) <u>technological advancements</u>, we built the International Space Station. The astronauts who work on the Station are able to do experiments that aren't possible on the earth due to the difference in gravity.

Words and Expressions

interplanetary *adj.* between planets 星际的

align *v.* to arrange 排列

coincide *v.* to meet or intersect 与……连接（或交叉）

approximate *adj.* rough 大约

exoplanet *n.* a planet that orbits a star outside the solar system 系外行星

dwarf *n.* a particular kind of star which is quite small and not very bright 矮星

prominent *adj.* important or well known 重要的；著名的

headset *n.* a small pair of headphones 耳机

laptop *n.* a small portable computer 笔记本电脑

Notes

Enceladus   the sixth largest satellite of Saturn 土卫二

With the recent growth of interests in space, we've seen aerospace companies developing space planes to create an industry in space tourism. We've seen NASA announced findings of planets, moons and solar systems, and we've even seen companies such as SpaceX pushing their vision of an interplanetary species. But what are the benefits of doing this? And is space exploration that important?

What lies beyond the earth isn't something all that new. From the dawn of civilization, humans have always been interested in space. We know that ancient Egyptian priests used the position of the sun to predict flooding and built temples that strategically allowed light in during certain parts of the year, and the Mayans aligned their cities to coincide with astronomical events. Exploration isn't just about curiosity. Exploration is necessary for advancement, whether that be for oneself or species. Because humans have explored, we have expanded our scientific knowledge. And because we have expanded our knowledge, our civilizations advance.

Despite mainly being empty, our exploration of space has provided us with an abundance of information. Over just the last few decades, we've determined the approximate age of the universe. We found water on Mars. In 1992, we detected the first exoplanets. Between the years of 2004 and 2005, we discovered three new dwarf planets in our solar system. In 2014, we discovered that Enceladus, one of Saturn's moons, was hiding an underwater ocean. There are several examples of this, but I think you get the point.

While these bits of information are interesting, the data can be used to study the universe, further, the machines we build and the methods we use to gather this information provide us with a more direct reward—technology, due to the specialized tools needed to explore space. Some prominent examples of this include camera phones, wireless headsets, memory foam computer mice and even laptops. Many of these examples have become items we use on a daily basis. You may even be using some of them right now. With the help of these technological advancements, we built the International Space Station. The astronauts who work on the Station are able to do experiments that aren't possible on the earth due to the difference in gravity.

Task ②B Watch the video clip again and answer the following questions.

Question ① What have aerospace companies been doing to promote space exploration?

They have been developing space planes to create an industry in space tourism.

Question ② What is the major significance of space exploration?

Space exploration has helped advance our civilizations by exploring and expanding our scientific knowledge. It has provided us with an abundance of information and technology.

Question ③ What are the achievements of human beings in space exploration? Do some research and share what you have found with your partner.

(This question is open-ended.)

▶ Speaking

Task 1 Work in groups and discuss the achievements humans recorded in space exploration, using some of the expressions listed below in your conversations.

What achievements have people made in space exploration from the dawn of civilization?	In ancient Egypt, priests used to … In …, we detected … Between … and …, we discovered …
What is the significance of space exploration?	Exploration is necessary for … We explore space because … The findings of space exploration can be used to …
What's your expectation toward space exploration?	I'm looking forward to … I believe … I hope that …

Task 2 Prepare a two-minute talk about space exploration, focusing on its progress and significance.

▶ Listening Skills

Learn to Distinguish Fact from Opinion

When listening for specific information on space exploration, pay attention to the difference between fact and opinion in order to discern the reliability and usefulness of information. The main difference between fact and opinion is that a fact is something that has actually happened or is something that is empirically true and can be supported by evidence whereas an opinion is a belief that is normally subjective or a belief that can vary based on a person's perspective, emotion, or individual understanding of something.

Fact Versus Opinion

Fact	Opinion
Something that has actually happened	A belief that is normally subjective
Something that is empirically true and can be supported by evidence	A belief that can vary based on a person's perspective, emotion, or individual understanding of something

Given below are some examples of facts:

> *China launched the crewed spacecraft Shenzhou-12 on Thursday.*
> *In 1992, we detected the first exoplanets.*
> *We discovered that Enceladus was hiding an underwater ocean.*
> *China launched the Chang'e-5 probe in 2020.*

Given below are some examples of opinions:

> *I think humans have always been interested in space.*
> *In my opinion, exploration isn't just about curiosity.*
> *Space exploration is very important.*
> *We can do better experiments on the earth than in the space lab.*

Practice

Listen to the following passages, try to distinguish facts from opinions and write down both in the table.

A: *China has found a perfect spot to build a world-class optical astronomy observatory! It's called Lenghu, or "Cold Lake"—a town in northwest China's Qinghai Province. It sits at an altitude of 4,200 to 4,500 meters. It has an extremely arid climate where 70 percent of the nights in a year have clear and photometric conditions. The median night temperature variation is only 2.4 degrees Celsius. That means it has stable surface air for observatory activities. Scientists say it will be built as part of a ground-based, high-quality observatory network, along with several others in the Eastern Hemisphere.*

Fact	Opinion
1. China has found a perfect spot to build a world-class optical astronomy observatory! 2. It's called Lenghu, or "Cold Lake"—a town in northwest China's Qinghai Province. 3. It sits at an altitude of 4,200 to 4,500 meters. 4. It has an extremely arid climate where 70 percent of the nights in a year have clear and photometric conditions. 5. The median night temperature variation is only 2.4 degrees Celsius.	Scientists say it will be built as part of a ground-based, high-quality observatory network, along with several others in the Eastern Hemisphere.

B: *After 1958, America launched many satellites for different usage such as reconnaissance satellites and meteorological satellites. All these satellites have influenced our daily life very much. Through them we can make our life safer and more wonderful.*

Fact	Opinion
After 1958, America launched many satellites for different usage such as reconnaissance satellites and meteorological satellites.	1. All these satellites have influenced our daily life very much. 2. Through them we can make our life safer and more wonderful.

Listening and Speaking: Development of Space Exploration

▶ Listening

Task 1   Listen to the conversation and fill in the chart with the information you get.

Situation: Here is a seminar on the history of space exploration.

Time	Programs of Space Exploration
In 1957	The Soviets launched the first (1) <u>artificial satellite</u>, Sputnik 1, into space.
In 1961	1. Soviet Yuri Gagarin became (2) <u>the first human</u> to orbit the earth in Vostok 1. 2. His flight lasted (3) <u>108 minutes</u>, and Gagarin reached 327 kilometers, about 202 miles.
In 1958	1. The first US satellite, Explorer 1, (4) <u>went into orbit</u>. 2. Both the Soviet Union and the United States have been (5) <u>making efforts to</u> land men on other planets.
In 1969	Astronaut Neil Armstrong took "one giant leap for mankind" as he stepped onto (6) <u>the moon</u>.
In the 1980s	1. Satellite communications expanded to carry (7) <u>television programs</u>. 2. People were able to (8) <u>pick up</u> the satellite signals on their home dish antennas.
In 1981	The launch of the space shuttle Columbia ushered in (9) <u>a period of reliance</u> on the reusable shuttle for most civilian and military (10) <u>space missions</u>.

Words and Expressions

orbital *adj.* connected with the orbit of a planet 轨道的
velocity *n.* the speed of sth. in a particular direction 速度
antenna *n.* a device that sends and receives television or radio signals 天线
space shuttle a spacecraft that is designed to travel between space and the earth 航天飞机

Scripts

Professor Lin: From the dawn of human civilizations, especially since the moon landing in the 1960s, humans have made big strides in space explorations. However, there is still so much about space we just don't know about yet. How did space travel and exploration begin? In today's seminar, we are going to discuss the history of space exploration. Any ideas?

Oscar: In the latter half of the 20th century, rockets became powerful enough to overcome the force of gravity to reach orbital velocities, paving the way for space exploration. On October 4, 1957, the Soviets launched the first artificial satellite, Sputnik 1, into space. Four years later, on April 12, 1961, Soviet Yuri Gagarin became the first human to orbit the earth in Vostok 1. His flight lasted 108 minutes, and Gagarin reached 327 kilometers, about 202 miles.

Professor Lin: Wonderful. At that time, both the Soviet Union and the United States were sending satellites into space. The first US satellite, Explorer 1, went into orbit on January 31, 1958. Since then, both countries have been making efforts to land men on other planets.

Lucy: Exactly. "Landing a man on the moon and returning him safely to the earth within a decade" was a national goal set by President John F. Kennedy in 1961. On July 20, 1969, astronaut Neil Armstrong took "one giant leap for mankind" as he stepped onto the moon.

Professor Lin: Yes, in the 1980s, satellite communications expanded to carry television programs, and people were able to pick up the satellite signals on their home dish antennas.

Oscar: Then what about space shuttles? I heard that people began to launch space shuttles in the 1980s.

Professor Lin: To be more specific, in April 1981, the launch of the space shuttle Columbia ushered in a period of reliance on the reusable shuttle for most civilian and military space missions. Since then, space systems have become more integral to homeland defense, weather surveillance, communication, navigation, imaging, and remote sensing for chemicals, fires, and other disasters.

Task 2 Listen to the passage and choose the best answer to each question you hear.

Situation: Here is an introduction of life inside China's space station.

(D) **1.** What do "taikonauts" refer to?

A. American astronauts.

B. Cosmos or astronauts.

C. Space or cosmos.

D. Chinese astronauts.

(B) **2.** What is the size of the core module?

A. 15 cubic meters.

B. 50 cubic meters.

C. 110 cubic meters.

D. 120 cubic meters.

(C) **3.** How do astronauts communicate with each other and the command center?

A. By using a spinning bike and other equipment.

B. By using a handheld terminal with an app.

C. By using bone conduction headphones.

D. By using a reserved private voice channel.

Words and Expressions

cosmos *n.* the universe 宇宙

spacious *adj.* (esp. of a room or building) having ample space 宽敞的

sanitation *n.* the process of keeping places clean and healthy 环境卫生

shredded *adj.* sliced 切碎的

spinning *n.* a type of exercise performed on an exercise bike 动感单车练习

treadmill *n.* an exercise device on which a person can walk or jog without changing the place 跑步机

The first three Chinese astronauts arrived at the country's space station with the Shenzhou-12 mission in mid-June. What is life like aboard the space station? How will China's astronauts live there? Let's take a look in this episode of *Tech Breakdown*.

You might have heard the word "taikonaut" in recent news reports. It is the term used to refer to Chinese astronaut. "Taikonaut" is a combination of the Chinese word "taikong", meaning space or cosmos, and astronaut.

Given the taikonauts will be staying in space for a relatively long time, efforts have been made to keep the space station as cozy as possible. The first thing was to provide them with a spacious living area.

The space station's core module is about 50 cubic meters in size, with three separate bedrooms and one bathroom. Combined with the two lab capsules, the living space is about 110 cubic meters, a huge upgrade compared to China's first space lab Tiangong-1, which is just 15 cubic meters. Inside the core module, six zones have been set up for the astronauts—for work, sleep, sanitation, dining, healthcare and exercise, all fully covered by Wi-Fi.

For the current mission, more than 120 kinds of cuisines have been prepared to ensure the taikonauts a balanced and nutritious diet. Such popular Chinese cuisines as Kung Pao chicken and Yuxiang shredded pork are on the menu.

There is also a "space gym" in the core module, equipped with a spinning bike, a treadmill and other equipment for astronauts to work out. Each taikonaut has a handheld terminal with an app to switch cabin lighting among work, sleep and exercise modes, according to their personal needs. And they use bone conduction headphones to communicate with each other and the command center. If they get homesick, a private voice channel has been reserved for them to call their families and friends on the earth.

The taikonauts on this latest mission will stay in space for three months to build the space station and conduct various other tasks. So, we can expect more about their lives in outer space in the coming days and weeks!

Questions

1. What do "taikonauts" refer to?

2. What is the size of the core module?

3. How do astronauts communicate with each other and the command center?

Task ③ Listen to the passage and fill in the blanks with the information you get.

Situation: Here is a talk about China's contribution to space exploration.

A critical element in China's 14th Five-Year Plan from 2021–2025 is the continued emphasis on technological advancement in achieving the goal of self-reliance, and (1) <u>progress in space exploration</u> is very much part of this.

Results are not automatic, but stem from long-term planning and hard work. China's lunar exploration program launched back in 2007 has led the country to (2) <u>undertake five missions</u> known as Chang'e, arithmetically numbered from one to five.

A 2016 white paper on space activities clarified Beijing's vision by mentioning its ambition of (3) <u>becoming a space power</u> in all aspects with the capabilities to make innovations independently, to (4) <u>make scientific discovery</u> and research at the cutting edge, to promote strong and sustained (5) <u>economic and social development</u>, to effectively and reliably (6) <u>guarantee national security</u>, to exercise sound and efficient governance, and to carry out mutually beneficial (7) <u>international exchanges and cooperation</u>.

Words and Expressions

lander *n.* a space vehicle designed to land on another planet 着陆器

retrieve *v.* to bring or get sth. back 取回

epicenter *n.* the very center of a thing 中心

module *n.* a unit of a spacecraft that can function independently of the main part 舱

dispatch *v.* to send 派遣

dock *v.* to join together in space 对接

in tandem with in cooperation with 合作

feat *n.* an action or a piece of work that needs skill, strength or courage 壮举

in regard to concerning 关于

span *v.* to extend 延伸

In 2018, Chang'e-4, consisting of a lander, a rover and a relay satellite, managed to successfully land on the far side of the moon. It was a (8) historic development that allowed original discoveries. It revealed impressive lunar images and information from a side of the moon not (9) explored by any other space power before. In December 2020, Chang'e-5 concluded China's first ever lunar material retrieving mission.

In an environment of uncertainty, what remains certain is China's determination to technologically progress—even in areas where it had previously lagged behind. China's miracle now (10) spans the space field.

A critical element in China's 14th Five-Year Plan from 2021–2025 is the continued emphasis on technological advancement in achieving the goal of self-reliance, and progress in space exploration is very much part of this.

Results are not automatic, but stem from long-term planning and hard work. China's lunar exploration program launched back in 2007 has led the country to undertake five missions known as Chang'e, arithmetically numbered from one to five.

A 2016 white paper on space activities clarified Beijing's vision by mentioning its ambition of becoming a space power in all aspects with the capabilities to make innovations independently, to make scientific discovery and research at the cutting edge, to promote strong and sustained economic and social development, to effectively and reliably guarantee national security, to exercise sound and efficient governance, and to carry out mutually beneficial international exchanges and cooperation.

In 2018, Chang'e-4, consisting of a lander, a rover and a relay satellite, managed to successfully land on the far side of the moon. It was a historic development that allowed original discoveries. It revealed impressive lunar images and information from a side of the moon not explored by any other space power before. In December 2020, Chang'e-5 concluded China's first ever lunar material retrieving mission.

In recent months, the country again became the epicenter of international attention for its space activity. China is methodically constructing its space station, named Tiangong, or Heavenly Palace. Tianhe module, which will function as the management and control hub of the space station, was launched in the end of April 2021. Less than two months later, Chinese astronauts were dispatched to Tiangong, their Shenzhou-12 spacecraft docking at the space station. Apart from their technical work, the Chinese astronauts completed a successful spacewalk.

In tandem with Tiangong, China had already managed to send a rover named Zhurong to Mars. Since mid-May, it has thus become only the third country, after the United States and the Soviet Union, to perform this feat in regard to the red planet. The Chinese operation yielded immediate results outlining the potential for new, impressive journeys.

In an environment of uncertainty, what remains certain is China's determination to technologically progress—even in areas where it had previously lagged behind. China's miracle now spans the space field.

Task 4 Listen to the passage and answer the following questions.

Situation: Here is additional information about pioneering works in space exploration.

Question 1 Why do people find it necessary to devise some practical means of countering the influence of Earth's gravity?

To translate the fictional images of space travel into reality.

Question 2 What's the influence of Konstantin E. Tsiolkovsky's work?

His work greatly influenced later space and rocket research in Europe.

Question 3 What's Hermann Oberth's contribution to space exploration?

His publications led to the creation of a number of rocket clubs in Germany as enthusiasts tried to turn his ideas into practical devices.

Notes

Konstantin E. Tsiolkovsky (1857.9.17–1935.9.19)   Russian inventor and rocket expert 康斯坦丁·E. 齐奥尔科夫斯基（俄罗斯发明家、火箭专家）

Robert Hutchings Goddard (1882.10.5–1945.8.10) American engineer, professor, physicist and inventor 罗伯特·哈金斯·戈达德（美国工程师、教授、物理学家和液体火箭的发明者）

Hermann Oberth (1894.6.25–1989.12.28)   German physicist, pioneer in rocketry 赫尔曼·奥伯特（德国物理学家、火箭先驱）

Jules Gabriel Verne (1828.2.8–1905.3.24)   French writer of the science fiction genre 儒勒·加布里埃尔·凡尔纳（法国科幻小说作家）

From the Earth to the Moon   a science fictional writing by Verne 《从地球到月球》（凡尔纳的科幻作品）

Wernher von Braun (1912.3.23–1977.6.16)   American Germany-born rocket scientist 沃纳·冯·布劳恩（美籍德裔火箭专家）

Apollo 11   the NASA program that resulted in American astronauts making a total of 11 spaceflights and walking on the moon 阿波罗 11 号（美国国家航空航天局的阿波罗计划，该计划总共执行了 11 次太空飞行任务，并成功登月）

Words and Expressions

fictional *adj.* imaginary 虚构的

devise *v.* to invent 发明

counter *v.* to do sth. to reduce 抵消

lay out   to explain or present sth. clearly 阐述

sophisticated *adj.* advanced 高水平的

rocketry *n.* the branch of science that deals with rockets and rocket propulsion 火箭学

Scripts

Since ancient times, people have studied the heavens and used their observations and explanations of astronomical phenomena for both religious and practical purposes. They dreamed of leaving the earth to explore other worlds by describing fictional journeys to the moon and the sun. In order to translate these fictional images of space travel into reality, people find it necessary to devise some practical means of countering the influence of the earth's gravity. By the beginning of the 20th century, there had been pioneering work done by Konstantin E. Tsiolkovsky, Robert Hutchings Goddard and Hermann Oberth.

Konstantin E. Tsiolkovsky studied in detail the use of rockets for spaceflight. As a Russian schoolteacher and mathematician, he published an article "Exploration of Cosmic Space by Means of Reaction Devices" in 1903 which laid out many of the principles of spaceflight. Up to his death in 1935, Tsiolkovsky continued to publish sophisticated studies on the theoretical aspects of spaceflight. He never complemented his writings with practical experiments in rocketry, but his work greatly influenced later space and rocket research in Europe.

Robert Hutchings Goddard was an American scientist who became interested in space exploration after reading works such as *The War of the Worlds*. In the 1920s, as a professor of physics at Clark University in Worcester, Massachusetts, Goddard began to experiment with liquid-fueled rockets. His first rocket, launched in Auburn, Massachusetts, on March 16, 1926, rose 12.5 meters and traveled 56 meters from its launching place. The noisy character of his experiments made it difficult for Goddard to continue work in Massachusetts. With support from others, he moved to Roswell, New Mexico, where from 1930 to 1941 he built engines and launched rockets of increasing complexity.

The third widely recognized pioneer of rocketry, Hermann Oberth, was by birth a Romanian but by nationality a German. Reading Jules Gabriel Verne's *From the Earth to the Moon* as a youth inspired him to study the requirements for interplanetary travel. His publications led to the creation of a number of rocket clubs in Germany as enthusiasts tried to turn his ideas into practical devices. The most important of these groups historically was the *Society for Spaceship Travel*, which had as a member the young Wernher von Braun. Although Oberth's work was crucial in stimulating the development of rocketry in Germany, he himself had only a limited role in that development. Alone among the rocket pioneers, Oberth lived to see his ideas become reality: He was Braun's guest at the launch of Apollo 11 on July 16, 1969.

Speaking

Task 1 Work in groups and discuss China's contribution to space exploration in detail, using some of the expressions listed below in your conversations.

Can you briefly describe the development of China's space exploration?	From ..., China put emphasis on ... In ..., the country undertook ... In ..., China further clarified the target of ...
Can you describe the Tiangong space station?	The Tiangong space station program was launched in ... The space station functions as ... The space station's core module is ...
Can you describe China's plan on space exploration?	In tandem with Tiangong, China managed to ... China is determined to ... China's operation will contribute to ...

Task 2 Prepare a two-minute talk about the development of space exploration. You may have a discussion with your classmates first and then formulate the talk.

▶ Communication Skills

Learn to Talk About Space Exploration

There are various ways to talk about space exploration. One of them may include the following steps:

1. **Introduce the type of space exploration.**

   - We are now interested in ...
   - The most studied planet in the solar system is ...
   - The planet under exploration is ...
   - What attracts us in the solar system is ...

2. **Describe the discoveries of space exploration.**

   - Scientists have found ...
   - It is the ... smallest planet ...
   - Its diameter is ...
   - Its surface area/temperature is ...

3. **Assess the significance of space exploration.**

   - We find it very significant to ...
   - The exploration is necessary for ...
   - The exploration has provided us with ...
   - The exploration might be the key to ...

Consolidating: Give a Talk About Space Exploration

Teaching Tips

1. Familiarize students with the purpose of this section—practicing the communication skills.
2. Call students' attention to the expressions denoting the outline of the talk about space exploration.
3. Have students work in groups of four, make a 5-minute video to talk about space exploration (one student working as the photographer and the other three taking turns talking about space exploration) and then upload the video onto the online learning platform for class sharing and constructive feedback.

Listen to the passage, fill in the blanks with the information you get, and then use them as the outline to make a video to introduce space exploration.

I. Exploration of Mars

　　1. Mars is the most studied planet in (1) the solar system after the earth.

　　2. We still have much to learn about (2) the red planet.

II. Discoveries of Mars

　　1. It is the (3) fourth planet from the sun and the second smallest planet in the solar system.

　　2. Its diameter is almost (4) the width of Africa.

　　3. Its surface area (5) is similar to that of all of the earth's continents combined.

　　4. Just like the earth, Mars is (6) a rocky planet.

　　5. Mars is dry, (7) barren and cold, and its temperature can be as low as (8) minus 142 degrees Celsius.

　　6. Scientists have found (9) lake beds and river valleys on Mars, showing us where (10) water once flowed.

　　7. Mars also has volcanoes, such as Olympus Mons, which is (11) three times the height of Mount Everest and was once active.

　　8. Water can still be found on Mars in the form of (12) polar ice caps.

III. Significance of Mars Exploration

　　1. Scientists hope to discover that the planet can (13) support life once again.

　　2. Some people even think that life on Mars might be the key to (14) a bright new future for humanity.

Mars is the most studied planet in the solar system after the earth. Today, NASA and other space programs are working to send people to Mars. However, we still have much to learn about the red planet.

Scientists believed Mars was formed about 4.5 billion years ago. It is the fourth planet from the sun and the second smallest planet in the solar system. Its diameter is almost the width of Africa. And its surface area is similar to that of all of Earth's continents combined. Just like the earth, Mars is a rocky planet. The ancient Romans named the planet Mars after their God of War because of its blood-red appearance. We all know that Mars is red because it is covered with red dust. Today, Mars is dry, barren and cold. Its temperature can be as low as minus 142 degrees Celsius. But scientists think that billions of years ago, Mars was much warmer and had liquid water on its surface. Scientists have found lake beds and river valleys on Mars, showing us where water once flowed. Mars also has volcanos, such as Olympus Mons, the largest volcano in the solar system. It is three times the height of Mount Everest and was once active. But about fifty million years ago, all volcanic activities on Mars stopped. Water can still be found on Mars in the form of polar ice caps. Because of this, some scientists believe that life may have once existed on the red planet.

Since the 1960s, scientists from around the world have launched missions to Mars. They want to understand the planet, its past and its present. They hope to discover that the planet can support life once again. There are some who even think that life on Mars might be the key to a bright new future for humanity.

Practice

Work in groups to make a video about space exploration by using the communication skills you have learned in this unit and the outline of the above passage. You can also use some of the expressions in the sections of Listening and Watching which may help make your introduction both informative and interesting. Then upload the video onto the online learning platform for class sharing and constructive feedback.

Goal Checking: Reflect and Evaluate

Work in groups. Reflect on and evaluate what you have learned in this unit, following the directions below.

1. Watch the videos of talking about space exploration made by other groups and evaluate them according to the rubric given below.

> **The video is excellent because ...**
>
> - It describes space exploration in a detailed manner.
>
> - The use of expressions is idiomatic and the sentences are fluent and cohesive.
>
> - It is well designed, clearly organized and vivid in presentation.

2. Select the best video conforming to the rubric above, watch it again and write down as many words and expressions of the type, discoveries and significance of space exploration as you can to vote for the best presenter.

Type of Space Exploration	Discoveries of Space Exploration	Significance of Space Exploration
Total Points:	Total Points:	Total Points:

Unit 3
Cultural Taboos

- **Warming Up:** Think and Discuss Cultural Diversity

- **Watching and Speaking:** Development of Cultural Taboos

  Objective: Identify and describe development of cultural taboos

- **Listening and Speaking:** Different Cultural Taboos

  Objective: Identify and describe different cultural taboos

- **Consolidating:** Give a Talk About Cultural Taboos

  Objective: Talk about cultural taboos

- **Goal Checking:** Reflect and Evaluate

Do's Don'ts

ABOO

Unit 3

Teaching Tips

1. Familiarize students with the purpose of this section—arousing their interest in the topic of cultural taboos.
2. Ask if all the students have done the Warming Up exercises and check the answers in class.

Warming Up: Think and Discuss Cultural Diversity

Before you start this unit, finish the following exercises with a partner.

1. Listen to the news and discuss with a partner the significance of the World Day for Cultural Diversity for Dialogue and Development.

Keys

The World Day for Cultural Diversity for Dialogue and Development represents a precious opportunity to celebrate the essential role of cultural diversity as a key driver for peace and sustainable development.

2. What's the relation between cultural diversity and cultural taboos? Does understanding taboos of different cultures facilitate intercultural communication? Do some research and share what you have found with your partner.

Words and Expressions

inclusive *adj.* including a wide range of people, things, ideas, etc. 包容广阔的

implementation *n.* putting a decision or plan into effect 实施

Notes

UNESCO   United Nations Educational, Scientific and Cultural Organization 联合国教科文组织

On May 21, 2021, UNESCO and the European Broadcasting Union (EBU) joined forces to celebrate the World Day for Cultural Diversity for Dialogue and Development. Forty-four radio music channels across Europe, Canada, the US, Brazil, Australia and New Zealand broadcasted Music & the Spoken Word events to mark the occasion.

The World Day for Cultural Diversity for Dialogue and Development represents a precious opportunity to celebrate the essential role of cultural diversity as a key driver for peace and sustainable development. Three-quarters of the world's major conflicts have a cultural dimension. Bridging the gap between cultures is therefore urgent and necessary for peace and stability. Protecting and promoting cultural diversity is also integral to reducing inequalities and building more inclusive societies.

The media can play an essential role in promoting diverse cultural content on the radio and on the screen. Media diversity is also recognized as a key indicator for monitoring the implementation of the UNESCO 2005 Convention for the Protection and Promotion of the Diversity of Cultural Expressions.

Watching and Speaking: Development of Cultural Taboos

▶ Watching

Teaching Tips

1. Familiarize students with the purpose of this section—identifying cultural taboos in different countries and understanding how cultural taboos come into being.
2. Call students' attention to Words and Expressions, and Notes before watching.
3. Have students pay attention to the situation of each task.
4. Have students do the tasks and check the answers.

Task 1 A Watch the video clip and choose the best answer to each question you hear.

Situation: Lucy and Jessica are having a conversation about cultural taboos.

(C) **1.** Which number is regarded as bad luck in some European countries?
A. 4.
B. 11.
C. 13.
D. 15.

(B) **2.** What are people NOT allowed to do at a London dinner party?
A. To bring a prepared gift to the host.
B. To take off one's shoes when arriving.
C. To keep away from anything labeled 13.
D. To send the odd number of flowers.

(A) **3.** Why is taking shoes off when visiting friends regarded as polite behavior in some countries?
A. Because it keeps the bad luck outside.
B. Because it brings good luck to the host.
C. Because it can be an insult to the host.
D. Because it shows disrespect to the host.

▌*Words and Expressions*
fill in to supply information to sb. 向某人提供情况

▌Notes
Easter lily any of several white cultivated lilies that bloom in early spring 复活节百合

Scripts

Jessica: Hi Lucy, how are you?

Lucy: Hi Jessica, I'm doing well. I'm preparing for the final exam. How are you?

Jessica: I'm fine. Still working on my senior thesis, you know. Oh, you must be busy, aren't you? Which exam are you preparing for?

Lucy: Intercultural communication. I'm reviewing the cross-cultural taboos in different countries.

Jessica: That's an interesting topic! Fill me in.

Lucy: Sure thing! For example, numbers become taboo in some cultures. In the United States and some European countries, 13 is regarded as bad luck.

Jessica: I know! Some people try to avoid bad luck by keeping away from anything numbered or labeled thirteen.

Lucy: Exactly. Another example is that removing shoes or not when visiting friends is worth a second thought when you are in some countries. If you take off your shoes when arriving at the door of a London dinner party, the host will find you uncivilized. But if you don't remove your shoes before entering someone's home in Asia, Hawaii, or the Pacific Islands, you'll be considered disrespectful.

Jessica: Yes. Because it is believed that removing your shoes not only keeps sand and dirt out of the house, but also keeps the bad luck outside.

Lucy: And there are some other taboos in the world. For instance, in Egypt, don't add salt into the bowl when dishes have been presented to you because it is an insult to the cook. In Ukraine, if you intend to send flowers, you must ensure that the number of flowers is odd because the even number is sent to a funeral. And do not send yellow flowers or Easter lilies to others, because these kinds of flowers are only prepared for the funeral.

Jessica: Oh, wow, one certainly doesn't want to make the mistake of sending the wrong number or kind of flowers to the wrong occasions. Thanks, Lucy, and good luck with your final exam!

Questions

1. Which number is regarded as bad luck in some European countries?

2. What are people NOT allowed to do at a London dinner party?

3. Why is taking shoes off when visiting friends regarded as polite behavior in some countries?

Task 1 B Watch the video clip again and match the countries with the cultural taboos.

A. The US and some European countries
B. Asia, Hawaii and the Pacific Islands
C. Ukraine
D. The UK
E. Egypt

(D) **1.** Removing shoes before entering someone's home is considered uncivilized.

(A) **2.** Thirteen is regarded as bad luck.

(E) **3.** Don't add salt into the bowl when dishes have been presented to you because it is an insult to the cook.

(C) **4.** Do not send yellow flowers or Easter lilies to others, because these kinds of flowers are only prepared for the funeral.

(B) **5.** If you don't remove your shoes before entering someone's home, you'll be considered disrespectful.

Task **2** **A** Watch the video clip and fill in the blanks with the information you get.

Situation: Here is an introduction of how cultural taboos come into being.

Are you afraid of black cats? Would you open an umbrella indoors? And how do you feel about the (1) <u>number thirteen</u>? Whether or not you believe in them, you're probably (2) <u>familiar with</u> a few of these superstitions. So how did it happen that people in many parts of the world (3) <u>knock on wood</u>, or avoid stepping on sidewalk cracks? Well, although they have no basis in science, many of these weirdly specific beliefs and practices do have equally weird and (4) <u>specific origins</u>. Because they involve supernatural causes, it's no surprise that many superstitions are based on (5) <u>religion</u>. For example, knocking on wood is thought to (6) <u>come from</u> the folklore of the ancient Indo-Europeans or possibly people who predated them who believed that trees were home to (7) <u>various spirits</u>. And somehow, this tradition survived long after belief in these spirits had (8) <u>faded away</u>. And believe it or not, some superstitions actually make sense, or at least they did until we forgot their original purpose. For example, theater scenery used to (9) <u>consist of</u> large painted backdrops, raised and lowered by stagehands who would whistle to signal each other. Absentminded whistles from other people could (10) <u>cause an accident</u>. But the taboo against whistling backstage still exists today, long after the stagehands started using radio headsets.

Words and Expressions

superstition *n.* belief in things that are not real or possible 迷信

sidewalk *n.* a pavement 人行道

crack *n.* a narrow space or opening 裂纹；裂缝

weirdly *adv.* strangely 奇怪地

supernatural *adj.* not existing in nature or subject to explanation according to natural laws 超自然的

folklore *n.* the traditions and stories of a country or community 民间传说

predate *v.* to precede 早于

fade away to disappear slowly or secretly 逐渐消失

backdrop *n.* a painted clothing hung at the back of a theatre stage as part of the scene 背景幕布

stagehand *n.* a stage worker 舞台工作人员

absentminded *adj.* showing an inattentive disposition 心不在焉的

cling to to try to keep 墨守

outdated *adj.* out of date 过时的

irrational *adj.* not based on clear logical thought 不合逻辑的

home run a hit that allows the person hitting the ball to run around all the bases without stopping （棒球）本垒打

bias *n.* an interest or ability in one thing more than others 偏爱

illusion *n.* a false idea or belief 错觉

Scripts

Are you afraid of black cats? Would you open an umbrella indoors? And how do you feel about the number thirteen? Whether or not you believe in them, you're probably familiar with a few of these superstitions. So how did it happen that people in many parts of the world knock on wood, or avoid stepping on sidewalk cracks? Well, although they have no basis in science, many of these weirdly specific beliefs and practices do have equally weird and specific origins. Because they involve supernatural causes, it's no surprise that many superstitions are based on religion. For example, knocking on wood is thought to come from the folklore of the ancient Indo-Europeans or possibly people who predated them who believed that trees were home to various spirits. And somehow, this tradition survived long after belief in these spirits had faded away. And believe it or not, some superstitions actually make sense, or at least they did until we forgot their original purpose. For example, theater scenery used to consist of large painted backdrops, raised and lowered by stagehands who would whistle to signal each other. Absentminded whistles from other people could cause an accident. But the taboo against whistling backstage still exists today, long after the stagehands started using radio headsets.

So why do people cling to these bits of forgotten religions, coincidences and outdated advice? Aren't they being totally irrational? Well, yes, but for many people, superstitions are based more on cultural habits than conscious beliefs. After all, no one is born knowing to avoid walking under ladders or whistling indoors, but if you grow up being told by your family to avoid these things, chances are they'll make you uncomfortable, even after you logically understand that nothing bad will happen. And since doing something like knocking on wood doesn't require much effort, following the superstition is often easier than consciously resisting it. Besides, superstitions often do seem to work. Maybe you remember hitting a home run while wearing your lucky socks. This is just our psychological bias at work. You're far less likely to remember all the times you struck out while wearing the same socks. But believing that they work could actually make you play better by giving you the illusion of having greater control over events. So in situations where confidence can make a difference, like sports, those crazy superstitions might not be so crazy after all.

Task **2** **B** Watch the video clip again and answer the following questions.

Question **1** What do people think is the basis of superstitions?

For many people, superstitions are based more on cultural habits than conscious beliefs.

Question **2** What are the reasons why people cling to certain cultural habits?

There are two reasons: first, some people grow up being told by their family to avoid doing certain things; second, some habits don't require much effort and following the superstition is often easier than consciously resisting it.

Question **3** What are the origins of cultural taboos in your culture? Select one taboo as an example to discuss with your partner.

(This question is open-ended.)

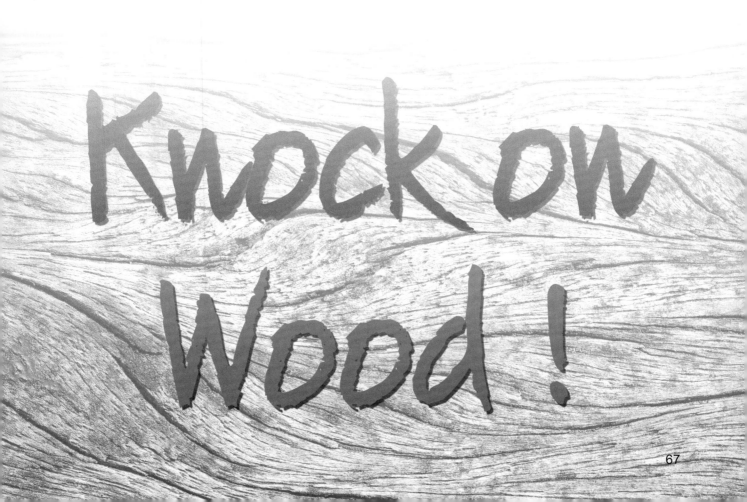

▶ Speaking

Task 1 Work in groups to discuss taboos in your culture and their origins, using some of the expressions listed below in your conversations.

What are the taboos in your culture?	... becomes a taboo in my culture. In my culture, ... is regarded as a taboo. There are some other taboos such as ...
What are the origins of the taboos in your culture?	They are based on ... It is believed that ... They are just psychological biases at ...

Task 2 Prepare a two-minute talk about the cultural taboos and their origins, explaining why there are such taboos and what influence they exert on our daily life.

Task 2 Listen to the passage and choose the best answer to each question you hear.

Situation: Here is an introduction of color taboos around the world.

(A) 1. What does red represent in Western cultures?
   A. Excitement and passion.
   B. Happiness and fortune.
   C. Prosperity and fortune.
   D. Luck and prosperity.

(C) 2. Which of the following statements about orange is NOT true?
   A. It reminds people of autumn and harvest.
   B. It is associated with frivolity and amusement.
   C. It represents the veil between worlds.
   D. It is the color of the god of wine-making's robes in mythological paintings.

(A) 3. What does green represent in South America?
   A. Nature, spring and good health.
   B. Love, passion and good luck.
   C. Love, anger and poor health.
   D. Anger, sickness and bad luck.

Notes

Halloween the night of the 31st of October and is traditionally said to be the time when ghosts and witches can be seen (On Halloween, children often dress up as ghosts and witches) 万圣节前夕（10 月 31 日晚，传说此时可见鬼巫，当晚儿童常化装成鬼巫尽情玩闹）

Bacchus God of wine and plants in Roman mythology 巴克科斯（罗马神话中的酒神和植物神）

Words and Expressions

have the blues to be in the state of being sad 忧愁

intangible *adj.* not having physical presence 无形的

anthropology *n.* the study of what makes us human 人类学

symbolism *n.* the use of symbols in order to represent something 象征

symbology *n.* the study or interpretation of symbols 符号学

ingrained *adj.* deep-seated 根深蒂固的

invoke *v.* to cause sb. to have the feeling 唤起

arresting *adj.* very attractive 有吸引力的

dim *adj.* weak 微弱的

pumpkin *n.* a large round vegetable with thick orange skin 南瓜

veil *n.* sth. that hides or partly hides a situation or activity 遮蔽物

frivolity *n.* behavior that is silly or amusing 轻浮的举止

clown *n.* an entertainer who wears funny clothes and does silly things to make people laugh 小丑

wig *n.* a covering of false hair 假发

mythological *adj.* connected with ancient myths 神话的

robe *n.* a loose piece of clothing 长袍

conversely *adv.* in a way that is the opposite or reverse of sth. 反过来

discoloration *n.* the act of changing the natural color of something 褪色

nauseate *v.* to make sb. feel that they want to vomit 使人作呕

Scripts

If you've ever had the blues or have been so angry when you saw red, then you're familiar with the powerful ways in which color can describe intangible ideas and emotions. In art and anthropology, color symbolism refers to colors' ability to signify meaning to a viewer. While there are some universal associations people tend to have with a specific color, the symbology is often socially ingrained. Color meanings thus differ dramatically from culture to culture. Colors favored by a culture may be a taboo in another culture. Now, let's explore color taboos.

As a representative of both heat and heart, red invokes strong feelings in both positive and negative senses. It's a color universally considered to be arresting. In Western cultures, red also symbolizes excitement, passion, love and danger. It's the color that the Lady in Red wears, a woman who is not to be trusted. In China, red represents happiness, good fortune, luck and prosperity. Since it's such an auspicious color, people traditionally wear it for big celebrations such as the New Year. At weddings, brides wear red.

Orange is the color easiest to be seen in dim light. In the West, orange tends to bring to mind autumn and harvest, the changing leaves and a candle's glow in a pumpkin's carved smile. When paired with black, it represents Halloween, a time when the veil between worlds is supposedly thin. The Western world also associates orange with frivolity and amusement. Clowns often wear orange wigs. Mythological paintings traditionally depict Bacchus—the god of wine-making, fertility, ritual madness and happiness—in orange robes.

In North and South America, Europe and Islamic countries, surveys have shown that green is most commonly associated with nature, spring and good health. Conversely, some people in the United States and European Union sometimes associate it with poor health. The saying "green around the gills" refers to someone who appears sick. Although the origin of the phrase is lost, it's likely due to the discoloration of one's skin when they are nauseated.

Questions

1. What does red represent in Western cultures?
2. Which of the following statements about orange is NOT true?
3. What does green represent in South America?

Task ❸ Listen to the passage and fill in the blanks with the information you get.

Situation: Here is a talk about naming taboos around the world.

The trend for choosing an English name is nothing new. Adopting an English name shows a willingness to (1) <u>integrate into new life</u>, bridging the gap between two cultures. However, the process of choosing a name is open to unintended consequences which can unwittingly result in (2) <u>funny or potentially embarrassing names</u>.

Many students choose (3) <u>old fashioned</u>, unusual names which they may have read in an old book or seen in an old film. Trends in names change over time, so if you choose a name which is (4) <u>not commonly used</u> today, it will sound strange and out of place. For English people, the name "Mildred", most popular in 1913, conjures up images of old ladies in cardigans with (5) <u>curly white hair</u>. The name "Norman", most popular in 1931, suggests old men with walking sticks and flat caps.

Names such as "Harry" from *Harry Potter* or "Tom" from *Tom and Jerry* are fine because they are (6) <u>common English names</u>. If you like the idea of naming yourself after a fictional character, just check that is a commonly used English name (7) <u>before you commit</u>.

Another trend we have seen is students naming themselves after inanimate objects such as (8) <u>food items</u>. Even if you really love food, the names "Pizza" or "Cheese" are totally inappropriate, not least because your taste in food may change as you get older!

English words such as "easy" or "yes" do not make good names. (9) <u>Apart from</u> being unconventional, "easy" is a word sometimes used to describe females in a derogatory fashion. Calling yourself "Yes" (10) <u>leaves you open to</u> many confused conversations where you are unsure whether people are agreeing with you or addressing you!

Words and Expressions

unintended *adj.* not intended 无意的
unwittingly *adv.* without knowledge or intention 无意地
conjure up to suggest a mental picture of 使想起
cardigan *n.* a knitted woolen sweater 开襟羊毛衫
inappropriate *adj.* not appropriate 不恰当的
derogatory *adj.* expressive of a low opinion 贬义的

Scripts

Many international students choose an English nickname when they come to an English speaking country. Lots of the names are conventional, though others are not. Devil, Pizza, Ketchup, Batman, Cheese—you name it, we've heard it.

The trend for choosing an English name is nothing new. Adopting an English name shows a willingness to integrate into new life, bridging the gap between two cultures. However, the process of choosing a name is open to unintended consequences which can unwittingly result in funny or potentially embarrassing names.

Many students choose old fashioned, unusual names which they may have read in an old book or seen in an old film. Trends in names change over time, so if you choose a name which is not commonly used today, it will sound strange and out of place. For English people, the name "Mildred", most popular in 1913, conjures up images of old ladies in cardigans with curly white hair. The name "Norman", most popular in 1931, suggests old men with walking sticks and flat caps.

Names such as "Harry" from *Harry Potter* or "Tom" from *Tom and Jerry* are fine because they are common English names. If you like the idea of naming yourself after a fictional character, just check that is a commonly used English name before you commit.

Another trend we have seen is students naming themselves after inanimate objects such as food items. Even if you really love food, the names "Pizza" or "Cheese" are totally inappropriate, not least because your taste in food may change as you get older!

English words such as "easy" or "yes" do not make good names. Apart from being unconventional, "easy" is a word sometimes used to describe females in a derogatory fashion. Calling yourself "Yes" leaves you open to many confused conversations where you are unsure whether people are agreeing with you or addressing you!

Task 4   Listen to the passage and answer the following questions.

Situation: Here is a report about taboos in giving gifts.

Question ❶ What gift did Mark present at the Chinese colleague's wedding?

A small decorative gift.

Question ❷ What does giving shoes to friends imply in China?

It implies the presenter wants the recipient to walk away, or disappear.

Question ❸ What gifts do people present in business relations in both China and the US?

Fine whiskey and quality wines.

Words and Expressions

decorative *adj.* intended to look attractive or pretty 装饰性的

Scripts

When Mark Levine, an English-language instructor at Minzu University of China, was first invited to attend a Chinese colleague's wedding in Jiangsu Province in 2006, his second year in China, the California native was ready to present a small decorative gift for the new couple as he used to do in the United States.

However, his gesture suddenly seemed inappropriate as he realized the Chinese at the ceremony had red envelopes filled with cash to present rather than a packed gift.

"It's a little bit embarrassing when you present something that people didn't expect to receive on certain occasions," said Levine, who used to be a social worker in the US.

"In the US, people do that—give cash—as well but only for close relatives. People would normally give things as presents, while here in China red envelopes are more commonly welcomed." It was the first time the 66-year-old discovered the etiquette—including taboos—in gift giving.

Because of the existence of many homophones in Chinese, where words have the same pronunciation but different meanings, the process of gift selection is more elaborate in China than in the West because the same gifts can carry very different meanings. For example, giving shoes to friends is totally acceptable in the West, whereas in China it implies that the presenter wants the recipient to walk away, or disappear. However, some things are good gifts just about anywhere in the world. For example, in business relations, fine whiskey and quality wines are relatively safe gifts.

"Gift-giving is just one small part of Chinese culture that Westerners need to learn about. You can't learn everything in a day—you have to experience it to really learn the customs—but at least make an effort," said Dreyer, a British citizen who has lived and worked in China since 2007.

▶ Speaking

Task What have you learned from the taboos mentioned in the Listening Section? Work in groups and discuss what taboos you know, using some of the expressions listed below in your conversations.

Can you briefly describe the gesture taboos around the world?	Gestures that we use on a daily basis might mean ... In ..., the simple hand signal may convey ... In ..., the action of ... is considered a huge sign of ...
Can you describe the color taboos around the world?	Color meanings differ dramatically from culture to culture. As a representative of ..., red/orange/green ... is considered to be ... In ..., white/black/blue ... is associated with ...
Can you describe naming taboos around the world?	The process of choosing a name is open to ... You should check whether the name is ... A name most popular in the past may conjure up images of ...
Can you describe taboos of giving gifts around the world?	It's a little bit embarrassing when you present ... The process of gift selection is more elaborate in ... than in ... The relatively safe gifts in ... are ...

Task  Prepare a two-minute talk about different cultural taboos. You may have a discussion with your classmates first and then formulate the talk.

▶ Communication Skills

Learn to Talk About Cultural Taboos

There are various ways to talk about cultural taboos. One of them may include the following steps:

1. **Introduce the type of the taboo.**

   - People are not allowed to ...
   - People abstain from ...
   - ... is considered as a taboo.
   - One of the taboos is ...

2. **Explain the reasons behind the taboo.**

   - The reasons behind this taboo are ...
   - This taboo arises from ...
   - It's the ... that leads to ...
   - This taboo is based on the belief that ...

3. **Illustrate the cultural differences.**

   - Taboos vary from ...
   - One culture's taboo may not be ...
   - People differ in ...
   - People in ... consider ... to be a taboo.

Consolidating: Give a Talk About Cultural Taboos

Teaching Tips

1. Familiarize students with the purpose of this section—practicing the communication skills.
2. Call students' attention to the expressions denoting the outline of the talk about cultural taboos.
3. Have students work in groups of four, make a 5-minute video to talk about cultural taboos (one student working as the photographer and the other three taking turns talking about cultural taboos) and then upload the video onto the online learning platform for class sharing and constructive feedback.

Listen to the passage, fill in the blanks with the information you get, and then use them as the outline to make a video to introduce cultural taboos.

I. Introduction of Food Taboos

1. Across the world, people abstain from (1) consuming certain food and drink for a variety of reasons.

2. When these reasons are primarily based on (2) tradition and social norms, as opposed to personal choice based on factors such as taste or ethics, they can be said to constitute a food taboo.

II. Reasons Behind Food Taboos

1. Certain foods are avoided because of (3) religious restrictions.

2. Food taboos arise from (4) a misunderstanding of the way a particular animal or plant behaves, leading these foods to be considered unclean or unhealthy.

3. Sometimes, there may be (5) widespread superstition about a particular food, leading to a taboo against its consumption.

4. Occasionally, it's not an individual food, but (6) a particular combination of foods that is taboo.

III. Illustrations of Food Taboos

1. In India, eggs are among several foods that some communities (7) <u>are forbidden from eating</u> due to religious factors.

2. Many people in Western Africa believe that women in particular shouldn't eat eggs or they will (8) <u>become sterile</u>.

3. In Brazil, seafood is widely consumed, but a few communities consider (9) <u>certain fish to be taboo</u>.

4. For most of us, (10) <u>eating rats</u> is itself taboo; however, rat meat is a dietary staple for many communities around the world, including some in India, Vietnam, Ghana and the United States.

Scripts

Across the world, people abstain from consuming certain food and drink for a variety of reasons. When these reasons are primarily based on tradition and social norms, as opposed to personal choice based on factors such as taste or ethics, they can be said to constitute a food taboo.

The reasons behind food taboos vary. Sometimes certain foods are avoided because of religious restrictions. At other times, food taboos arise from a misunderstanding of the way a particular animal or plant behaves, leading these foods to be considered unclean or unhealthy. Sometimes, there may be widespread superstition about a particular food, leading to a taboo against its consumption. In some cases, there may have once been a good reason to avoid a particular food, and although the reason no longer applies and has been lost in the mists of history, the taboo persists. Occasionally, it's not an individual food, but a particular combination of foods that is taboo.

In the area of food, saying that something is unusual is always rather subjective, and this general rule applies even more to food taboos. One culture's food taboo can be and often is another culture's delicacy. Nonetheless, here are a few food taboos from around the world that many people are likely to find quite surprising.

In India, eggs are among several foods that some communities are forbidden from eating due to religious factors. Many people in Western Africa believe that women in particular shouldn't eat eggs or they will become sterile. Some believe that consumption of eggs is harmful for children too. It is claimed that this latter taboo was originally invented as a way to keep children from raiding village hens, disturbing and disrupting them, and eating too many eggs, but this origin story is likely to be apocryphal. A similar taboo against children eating eggs exists in Nigeria, and is based on the belief that consumption of eggs will make children steal.

In Brazil, seafood is widely consumed, but a few communities consider certain fish to be taboo. These include bottom feeding fish and carnivorous fish like piranhas, although the latter are quite popular in many parts of South America. In particular, people who are already unwell are advised not to eat these foods.

For most of us, eating rats is itself taboo; however, rat meat is a dietary staple for many communities around the world, including some in India, Vietnam, Ghana and the United States.

Practice

Work in groups to make a video about food taboos by using the communication skills you have learned in this unit and the outline of the above passage. You can also use some of the expressions in the sections of Listening and Watching which may help make your introduction both informative and interesting. Then upload the video onto the online learning platform for class sharing and constructive feedback.

Goal Checking:
Reflect and Evaluate

Work in groups. Reflect on and evaluate what you have learned in this unit, following the directions below.

1. Watch the videos of talking about cultural taboos made by other groups and evaluate them according to the rubric given below.

The video is excellent because ...

- It describes the cultural taboo in a detailed manner.

- The use of expressions is idiomatic and the sentences are fluent and cohesive.

- It is well designed, clearly organized and vivid in presentation.

2. Select the best video conforming to the rubric above, watch it again and write down as many words and expressions of cultural taboos as you can to vote for the best presenter.

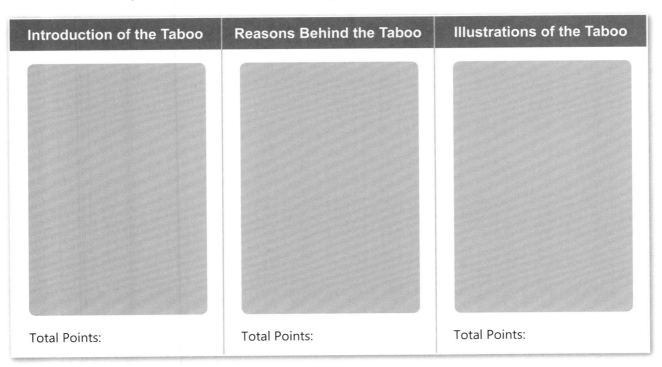

Introduction of the Taboo	Reasons Behind the Taboo	Illustrations of the Taboo
Total Points:	Total Points:	Total Points:

Unit 4

Disasters and Accidents

- **Warming Up:** Think and Discuss Resilience to Natural Disasters

- **Watching and Speaking:** Introduction of Disasters and Accidents
  Objective: Identify and describe different disasters and accidents

- **Listening and Speaking:** Coping with Disasters and Accidents
  Objective: Identify and describe how to cope with disasters and accidents

- **Consolidating:** Give a Talk About Disasters and Accidents
  Objective: Talk about disasters and accidents

- **Goal Checking:** Reflect and Evaluate

Teaching Tips

1. Familiarize students with the purpose of this section—arousing their interest in the topic of disasters and accidents.
2. Ask if all the students have done the Warming Up exercises and check the answers in class.

Warming Up: Think and Discuss Resilience to Natural Disasters

Before you start this unit, finish the following exercises with a partner.

1. Listen to the news and discuss with a partner why in recent decades, fewer people have been dying of natural hazards such as cyclones and floods.

Keys

More robust warning systems and responsive protection mechanisms have been put in place. In addition, governments have started to appreciate the importance of dealing with disaster risk in an integrated way rather than just responding on a hazard-by-hazard basis.

2. How can we prevent and mitigate natural disasters? Do some research and share what you have found with your partner.

Words and Expressions

cyclone *n.* a violent tropical storm in which strong winds move in a circle 龙卷风

hazard *n.* danger or risk 危险

fatality *n.* a death caused by an accident or by violence 死亡

robust *adj.* strong and not likely to fail 强劲的

livelihood *n.* a means of earning money in order to live 生计

exacerbate *v.* to make sth. worse 使……恶化

scenario *n.* the way in which a situation may develop 设想；预测

cascading risks risks which happen like water pouring downwards very fast and in large quantities 连锁风险

Scripts

The human and economic impacts of disasters, including biological ones, and climate change are documented in our "2021 Asia-Pacific Disaster Report". It demonstrates that climate change is increasing the risk of extreme events like heatwaves, heavy rain and flooding, drought, tropical cyclones and wildfires. Heatwaves and related biological hazards in particular are expected to increase in East and Northeast Asia, while South and Southwest Asia will encounter intensifying floods and related diseases.

However, in recent decades, fewer people have been dying as a result of other natural hazards such as cyclones and floods. Fatality rate concerning these natural disasters has been reduced not only because more robust warning systems and responsive protection mechanisms have been put in place, but also because governments have started to appreciate the importance of dealing with disaster risk in an integrated way rather than just responding on a hazard-by-hazard basis.

Disasters threaten not just human lives but also livelihoods. And they are likely to be even more costly in the future as their impacts are exacerbated by climate change. Annual losses from both natural and biological hazards across Asia and the Pacific are estimated at $780 billion. In a worst-case climate change scenario, the annual economic losses arising from these cascading risks could rise to $1.3 trillion.

Watching and Speaking: Introduction of Disasters and Accidents

▶ Watching

Teaching Tips

1. Familiarize students with the purpose of this section—identifying different disasters and accidents and understanding the prevention of disasters and accidents.
2. Call students' attention to Words and Expressions before watching.
3. Have students pay attention to the situation of each task.
4. Have students do the tasks and check the answers.

Task 1 A Watch the video clip and fill the names of disasters and accidents in appropriate columns.

Situation: Here is a seminar on disasters and accidents.

Disasters	Accidents
earthquake flood social conflict health epidemic industrial accident	falling down cutting choking poisoning burning

Words and Expressions

disrupt *v.* to upset 打乱；搅乱

subsist *v.* to survive 生存

induce *v.* to cause 引起；导致

alter *v.* to change 改变

epidemic *n.* a widespread outbreak of an infectious disease 流行病

count as to regard or be regarded as 视为

spawn *v.* to causes sth. to happen or to be created 引起

tsunami *n.* an extremely large wave in the sea caused by an earthquake 海啸

ascribe *v.* to consider that sth. is caused by a particular thing or person 把……归因于

Scripts

Professor: In this class, I'm going to invite some students to share with us information about unexpected things happening around us. Laura, could you please give us a brief introduction of unexpected things happening in daily life?

Laura: In our daily life, there are two types of unexpected things happening: disasters and home accidents.

Professor: What does disaster refer to?

Laura: A disaster is a consequence of a sudden disastrous event which seriously disrupts the normal function of the society or the community to the extent that it cannot subsist without outside help. No matter what society disasters occur in, they tend to induce change in government and social life. They may even alter the course of history by broadly affecting entire populations and exposing mismanagement or corruption regardless of how tightly information is controlled in a society.

Professor: Good, sounds like you've done your homework on the topic. Now, could you please provide us with some examples of disasters?

Laura: Of course. The occurrences of an event such as an earthquake, flood, social conflict, health epidemic or an industrial accident of any other events that negatively impacts human populations all count as disasters. Disasters are routinely divided into natural or human-made ones. A specific disaster may spawn a secondary disaster that increases the impact. A classic example is an earthquake that causes a tsunami, resulting in coastal flooding. Some manufactured disasters have been ascribed to nature.

Professor: Then what about home accidents? Is choking a home accident?

Laura: Yes. Choking is an accident that might happen, especially to children, at home. Actually, our home is the place where accidents are most likely to occur. Common home accidents include falling down, cutting, choking, poisoning and burning.

Professor: Exellent work, Laura. Now I'd like to invite Kevin to give us more details on disasters.

Task ❶ B Watch the video clip again and answer the following questions.

Question ❶ What is the definition of disaster?

A disaster is a consequence of a sudden disastrous event which seriously disrupts the normal function of the society or the community to the extent that it cannot subsist without outside help.

Question ❷ What are causes of disasters?

There are two kinds of causes: one is natural and the other is human-made.

Question ❸ How many home accidents do you know besides the ones mentioned in the video and how to prevent them?

(This question is open-ended.)

Task ② A Watch the video clip and describe the following four pictures (four steps of treating choking) with proper expressions.

Situation: Here is an introduction of how to treat choking.

Step 1: <u>cough it out</u>

Step 2: <u>give back blows</u>

Step 3: <u>give abdominal thrusts</u>

Step 4: <u>call 120</u>

Words and Expressions

casualty *n.* a person killed or injured in a war or in an accident 伤员；亡者

airway *n.* the passage by which air reaches a person's lungs 气道

blockage *n.* the state of being blocked 堵塞

starve of to keep sb. or sth. short of 使缺少

reassure *v.* to set sb's mind at rest 使……安心

shoulder blade a pair of large, flat, triangular-shaped bones on either side of the upper back 肩胛骨

abdominal *adj.* relating to the abdomen 腹部的

thrust *n.* a sharp hand gesture 推

breastbone *n.* a flat narrow bone in the middle of the chest 胸骨

obstruction *n.* sth. that blocks a passage or tube in your body 梗阻物

unresponsive *adj.* not reacting or responding 无反应的

commence *v.* to begin 开始

Scripts

Choking is a life-threatening situation and happens when the casualty's airway suddenly gets blocked so that they cannot breathe normally. Usually choking in small children is caused by a small foreign object whereas in adults it is most commonly food. If the blockage of the airway is mild, the casualty should be able to clear it by coughing. Any blockage of the airway should be taken very seriously as within a short time of the brain being starved of oxygen, brain damage can occur. Here are the recognition signs and symptoms: grasping of the throat, difficulty in speaking and breathing, persistent cough, pale grey or blue skin developing, or becoming unconscious.

Let's now look at the treatment. Once you have established that the casualties are in fact choking, your first action should be to calm and reassure the casualty and encourage them to cough. If this is not successful, you should stand behind the casualty, leading them slightly forward and supporting their upper chest with either one hand or your arm across their chest and give sharp back blows between their shoulder blades. These back blows should be attempted at a time. Check the mouth and remove any obstruction. If your back blows are unsuccessful, then you should attempt to give five abdominal thrusts. Again stand behind the casualty and place both arms around them leaning the casualty forward. Place one fist just below the breastbone and cut the fist with the other hand. Then pull sharply inwards and upwards to try and force the obstruction out.

If this is unsuccessful you should repeat the cycle of back blows and abdominal thrusts. And if after three cycles the obstruction is not cleared you should then call 120. If at any time the casualty becomes unresponsive and unconscious you should support the casualty to the floor, call the emergency services as soon as possible and commence basic life support.

Task ❷ B Watch the video clip again and answer the following questions.

Question ❶ What are the causes of choking in small children as well as adults?

Usually choking in small children is caused by a small foreign object whereas in adults it is most commonly food.

Question ❷ What are the recognition signs and symptoms of choking?

Grasping of the throat, difficulty in speaking and breathing, persistent cough, pale grey or blue skin developing, or becoming unconscious.

Question ❸ How do you prevent yourself and your family from choking? Do some research and share what you have found with your partner.

(This question is open-ended.)

▶ Speaking

Task ① Work in groups and discuss natural disasters, using some of the expressions listed below in your conversations.

What kinds of natural disasters do you know?	We have such natural disasters as … Now we are facing the risk of extreme events like … As far as I know, the common natural disasters we come across are …
What are the causes of these disasters?	The main cause of natural disasters is … Some natural disasters such as … are caused by … Some man-made disasters have been ascribed to …
What are the negative effects of these disasters?	Disasters threaten … They seriously disrupt the normal function of … The annual economic losses arising from them could rise to …

Task ② Prepare a two-minute talk about some accidents you know, focusing on their causes, features and treatment, and then deliver the speech in class.

ⓘ Listening Skills

Learn to Identify the Problem & Solution Pattern

When listening for specific information on disasters and accidents, pay attention to the problem & solution pattern used in the text, which typically consists of two parts— (1) problem: its causes and effects; and (2) solution. Being able to identify such a pattern helps you understand what is being talked about. Below is a T-chart on the topic of choking which shows the problem & solution pattern used in the text.

T-Chart

Problem	
• Cause	
• Effect	
Solution	

Practice

Listen to the following passage, try to identify the problem & solution pattern and take notes with the help of the following T-chart.

A boiling water burn is sometimes called a scald. It can also result from contact with steam.

More than 1 million people seek emergency treatment for burns each year in the United States, and about 10,000 die from burn-related infections.

The right care for a boiling water burn can ease the pain and reduce the risk of serious complications. After sustaining a boiling water burn, you must stop contact with the source of the burn as quickly as possible. If the hot water is on clothing, remove the clothing, unless it is stuck to the skin. Then you must cool the skin by running it under cold water for at least 10 minutes and do not put oils or any other products on the burn. If the burn is very painful and severe, or covers a large area of the body, you must seek emergency aid.

T-Chart

Problem	boiling water burn
• Cause	contact with steam
• Effect	More than 1 million people seek emergency treatment for burns each year in the United States; About 10,000 die from burn-related infections.
Solution	**After sustaining a boiling water burn:** 1. Stop contact with the source of the burn as quickly as possible; 2. Remove the clothing, unless it is stuck to the skin; 3. Cool the skin by running it under cold water for at least 10 minutes; 4. Do not put oils or any other products on the burn. **If the burn is very painful and severe, or covers a large area of the body:** Seek emergency aid.

Listening and Speaking: Coping with Disasters and Accidents

▶ Listening

Task 1 Listen to the conversation and decide whether each statement is T (true) or F (false).

Situation: Here is a seminar about home accidents.

(T) 1. The professor mentioned such potential hazards as hot water, household chemicals, fireplaces and sharp objects.

(T) 2. According to the professor, most non-fatal accidents are caused by falls from height.

(F) 3. Though homes can be dangerous, not many people require a hospital visit following an accident in the home.

(F) 4. The student's uncle once got food poisoning and he didn't make a full recovery until two weeks later.

(F) 5. The professor suggests that we should see a doctor at once when food poisoning happens.

Words and Expressions

slip *v.* to accidentally slide and lose your balance 滑倒

contaminated *adj.* made dirty or harmful 被污染了的

diarrhoea *n.* frequent and watery bowel movements 腹泻

cramp *n.* severe pain in the stomach （腹部）绞痛

chill *n.* an illness causing fever and shivering 畏冷

dehydration *n.* the excessive loss of body fluids 脱水

bland *adj.* not having a strong taste 清淡的

Scripts

Professor: Now let's move on to accidents, especially home accidents. There are many potential hazards in every home, such as hot water, household chemicals, fireplaces and sharp objects. All those factors may lead to serious home accidents. Most non-fatal accidents are caused by falls from height, with most deaths occurring as a result of fire.

Student A: Our home can be a dangerous place, you mean?

Professor: Exactly, especially for children under 5 years old. The home is the most common location for an accident to happen, with a lot of people requiring a hospital visit following an accident in the home. It is more important than ever to make sure that you are staying safe. For example, the design of some homes, such as those with marble floors, can also cause accidents because kids and older people can easily slip and fall on marble floors and get hurt.

Student A: I got it. So we should try to keep our home safe when designing homes and keep kids and old people away from dangerous places at home.

Professor: Another common home accident is food poisoning. Food poisoning is an illness caused by eating contaminated food. The main symptoms include feeling sick, vomiting, diarrhoea, stomach cramps and abdominal pain, a lack of energy and weakness, loss of appetite, fever, aching muscles and chills.

Student B: This reminds me of my uncle who once got the same symptoms after he ate contaminated food. As luck would have it, all these symptoms passed in a few days and he made a full recovery.

Professor: When food poisoning happens, you should rest and drink fluids to prevent dehydration until you feel better. Besides, you should eat when you feel up to it, but try small, light meals at first and stick to bland foods—such as toast, crackers, bananas and rice—until you begin to feel better.

Student B: Exactly. But I think the best way to prevent food poisoning from happening is not eating contaminated food.

Task ② Listen to the passage and choose the best answer to each question you hear.

Situation: Here is a talk about fire hazards at home.

(A) **1.** How much time do we have to escape safely when a house is on fire?
  A. Under two minutes.
  B. Over two minutes.
  C. Under five minutes.
  D. Over five minutes.

(B) **2.** What's the first tip given by the speaker?
  A. Keeping your children away from matches and lighters.
  B. Identifying and removing fire hazards in your home.
  C. Discussing safe meeting places outside your home.
  D. Practicing a fire escape plan with your family twice a year.

(A) **3.** What shouldn't you do if a fire does occur?
  A. Open a door to escape if it feels warm to the back of your hand.
  B. Use another exit or stay where you are if your exit route is blocked.
  C. Open a window and wave something white to signal for help.
  D. Stay low to the ground and crawl to avoid breathing in smoke.

Words and Expressions

precautionary *adj.* preventive 预防性的
pillowcase *n.* a removable cloth cover for a pillow 枕套

Scripts

As someone who has been a fire prevention engineer for almost 20 years, I can give a few simple but life-saving tips. Most people may not know this: when a house is on fire, we typically have only two minutes to escape safely. What we do before, during and after those two minutes can mean life and death. So, here are the tips.

First, you should prepare by identifying and removing fire hazards in your home. Anything that gets hot and catches fire easily needs plenty of space. There should be at least three feet between heating items and anything else that could catch fire. Turn off space heaters when not in use. You should always avoid smoking in bed. Don't leave candles lit when unattended or at bedtime.

Second, you should make sure your children know they should not play with fire, matches, or lighters. Keep matches and lighters in high or locked places away from children's reach.

Third, always remember to discuss safe meeting places outside your home and fire escape plan and practice with your family twice a year. Make sure everyone can get out safely in two minutes.

By taking those precautionary steps, we are off to a great start. But if a fire does occur, how to respond?

To begin with, do not open a door if it feels warm to the back of your hand. Warm or hot door temperatures could indicate that there is a fire on the other side. Use another exit instead. If your exit route is blocked, stay where you are. Open a window and wave something white to signal for help, such as a pillowcase or a piece of clothing.

Besides, stay low to the ground and crawl to avoid breathing in smoke. Follow your family's escape plan. Get out of the house, do not go back in, and call 119 and 120 right away. With these tips you'll be able to prevent fires and safely and quickly respond if there is one.

Questions

1. How much time do we have to escape safely when a house is on fire?

2. What's the first tip given by the speaker?

3. What shouldn't you do if a fire does occur?

Task ③ Listen to the passage and fill in the blanks with the information you get.

Situation: Here is a talk about an earthquake escape.

The day of the earthquake was the day before graduation when we were decorating the premises for the next day's celebrations. And we heard the early warning signal sent out by the Meteorological Agency to (1) <u>herald an imminent earthquake</u>. From that moment we had just seconds before the shaking began, slowly at first then ramping up to (2) <u>a terrifying violence</u>.

Adults were shouting at each other to switch off the gas supply, and we could hear the children (3) <u>screaming upstairs</u>. As I crouched on the floor under my desk my head kept thumping the underside of the table as the floor bucked beneath me. Through the window I could see the tops of the trees on the other side of the playing field (4) <u>shaking back and forth</u> with the force of the quake.

The shaking lasted six minutes—the longest six minutes of my life. I honestly thought that (5) <u>I was going to die</u>. Ours was the oldest school building in Sendai, and I couldn't help but (6) <u>imagine the whole thing</u> crumbling and collapsing into a pile of rubble. Many buildings actually did.

Words and Expressions

premises *n.* the buildings and land that an institution occupies in one place 办公场所

herald *v.* to be a sign that sth. is about to happen 预示将出现

imminent *adj.* likely to happen very soon 即将发生的

ramp sth. up to make sth. increase in amount 使……的数量增加

crouch *v.* to lower the body stance by bending the legs 蹲伏

thump *v.* to hit against sth. with a low loud sound 重击

buck *v.* to move up and down suddenly 猛烈颠簸

crumble *v.* to break or fall apart into very small pieces 破碎

rubble *n.* the pieces of brick, stone, or other materials 瓦砾

tremor *n.* shaking 颤抖

subside *v.* to become less strong or loud 减弱

evacuate *v.* to move people from a place of danger to a safer place 撤离；疏散

ensuing *adj.* following immediately and as a result of what went before 接踵而来的

in its own right because of its qualification, etc., not depending upon sth. else 独立地

magnitude *n.* the size of an earthquake 震级

apocalyptic *adj.* like the end of the world 像世界末日的

Thankfully ours didn't, and as the tremors subsided we were all (7) <u>evacuated safely to</u> the baseball field outside the school. There were three more aftershocks in the ensuing hour, so we were (8) <u>repeatedly thrown to</u> the ground as we gathered on the field. As we waited there in shock the sky began to fill with strange clouds and smoke, and it started to snow. Apocalyptic is the only way to describe it.

That night the school wouldn't allow me to go home because I (9) <u>lived alone</u>, so I stayed on the premises and helped as refugees from the surrounding areas began to arrive. We wouldn't have (10) <u>running water</u> or electricity for three days, so the facilities quickly became horrible.

❙Notes

the Meteorological Agency a Japanese government department supplying weather forecasts 日本气象厅

Scripts

The day of the earthquake was the day before graduation, and I was at the school where I taught English. It was a quarter to three and most of my pupils had gone home for the day, but some of the students and teachers were still there helping to decorate the premises for the next day's celebrations. I was heading downstairs to print something off in the classroom when I began to hear alarms going off on teachers' mobile phones—the early warning signal sent out by the Meteorological Agency to herald an imminent earthquake. From that moment we had just seconds before the shaking began, slowly at first then ramping up to a terrifying violence.

Adults were shouting at each other to switch off the gas supply, and we could hear the children screaming upstairs. As I crouched on the floor under my desk my head kept thumping the underside of the table as the floor bucked beneath me. Through the window I could see the tops of the trees on the other side of the playing field shaking back and forth with the force of the quake.

The shaking lasted six minutes—the longest six minutes of my life. I honestly thought that I was going to die. Ours was the oldest school building in Sendai, and I couldn't help but imagine the whole thing crumbling and collapsing into a pile of rubble. Many buildings actually did.

Thankfully ours didn't, and as the tremors subsided we were all evacuated safely to the baseball field outside the school. There were three more aftershocks in the ensuing hour—each one the size of a major earthquake in its own right, measuring up to 7.9 in magnitude—so we were repeatedly thrown to the ground as we gathered on the field. As we waited there in shock the sky began to fill with strange clouds and smoke, and it started to snow. Apocalyptic is the only way to describe it.

That night the school wouldn't allow me to go home because I lived alone, so I stayed on the premises and helped as refugees from the surrounding areas began to arrive. I had only been in Japan for six months at this point and couldn't speak much Japanese, so I was assigned a duty that didn't require much language skill: spraying people's hands with disinfectant after they used the bathroom. We wouldn't have running water or electricity for three days, so the facilities quickly became horrible.

Task 4 Listen to the passage and answer the following questions.

Situation: Here is a talk about how to cope with natural disasters.

Question 1 What emotions might you experience when a natural disaster takes place?

Shock, grief, sadness and despair.

Question 2 In what condition might strong emotions come back after the disaster has passed?

When there are significant reminders such as anniversaries or there is a threat of another natural disaster, these feelings might come back.

Question 3 Apart from keeping up your daily routine, what else can you do to recover from the experience of natural disasters?

It is helpful to let friends or family know how you're going, what you're thinking and feeling, and how you're coping with things.

Words and Expressions

turn upside down to turn sth. or sb. the other way up 把某物或某人倒过来

make sense of to understand 懂得

devastation *n.* great destruction or damage 毁坏

despair *n.* hopelessness 绝望

in a while later 稍后

Scripts

Sometimes we experience natural disasters. What if your world was turned upside down by a flood, fire or cyclone? How would you make sense of the devastation, the loss of friends, family, pets, your home and belongings? How might you feel if you'd been through something like this?

You may feel helpless like you couldn't do anything—waiting, not knowing. You may lose pretty much everything: your house, pets, photos. It's easier to say possessions don't matter as long as your family survived. But it isn't simple.

After a natural disaster you can experience a range of emotions like shock, grief, sadness and despair. You might be overwhelmed by feeling of powerlessness. You might feel guilty that you've survived if you know other people who didn't. And on top of these emotions, you might find everyday things like eating and sleeping become really difficult. These feelings and behaviors can go in a while after the disaster has passed. But you would usually expect strong emotions to start to settle after about six weeks. When there are significant reminders such as anniversaries or there is a threat of another natural disaster, these feelings might come back.

Recovery takes time and it's different for everyone. You might need some practical help with basic stuff like housing, school, travel and getting around. Or you might need help with how you cope with your thoughts and feelings. There are some things you can do for yourself that can really help. Try to keep up your normal daily routine like going to school or work, eating three meals a day, going to bed around the same time each night, and getting up around the same time each morning. It is helpful to let friends or family know how you're going, what you're thinking and feeling, and how you're coping with things. It can help you and others be aware of supports that might be helpful at different times.

Speaking

Task 1　What have you learned from the measures to take before, during and after disasters and accidents mentioned in the Listening Section? Work in groups and discuss how you feel and what you will do facing disasters and accidents, using some of the expressions listed below in your conversations.

Can you briefly describe how to prevent fire hazards at home?	First, we should prepare by ... Second, we should make sure that ... If a fire does occur, we should ...
Can you describe what to do when an earthquake happens?	When an earthquake takes place, we should ... As the tremors subside, we should ... When the early warning signal is sent out, we should crouch ...
Can you describe your feelings after you experience natural disasters?	I feel helpless/guilty as ... After a natural disaster, I can experience/might be overwhelmed by ... I might find everyday things ...

Task 2　Prepare a two-minute talk about the treatment of negative feelings and emotions after disasters or accidents. You may have a discussion with your classmates first and then formulate the talk.

▶ Communication Skills

Learn to Talk About Disasters and Accidents

There are various ways to talk about disasters or accidents. One of them may include the following steps:

1. **Describe the background of the disaster or accident.**

   - Years ago I ...
   - When I was doing ...
   - I was having a great time until I ...
   - I came across ... when I ...

2. **Describe how the disaster or accident occurred.**

   - As I approached ... I ...
   - Our bus/raft/boat/car collapsed because of ...
   - Right before I hit ...
   - The current was so strong that ...

3. **Describe how you dealt with the disaster or accident.**

   - At first, I was ... and then I ...
   - I took immediate action to ...
   - I yelled to ... but couldn't ...
   - I was eventually rescued by ...

Consolidating: Give a Talk About Disasters and Accidents

Listen to the passage, fill in the blanks with the information you get, and then use them as the outline to make a video to introduce a disaster or an accident.

I. Background of the Accident

1. Years ago we went on (1) <u>a family vacation</u> to Colorado and we went whitewater rafting with my sister and her family.

2. Everything was going along just fine. We were having a great time until we were (2) <u>approaching the halfway point</u>.

II. Occurrence of the Accident

1. Right (3) <u>in the middle of</u> the river was a boulder. As we approached that halfway point we broadsided that boulder in our raft. And it caused our raft (4) <u>to collapse</u>.

2. I went in the water and (5) <u>came up downstream</u> and I looked back thinking that I was the one that went in the water and my family didn't.

3. I saw (6) <u>a very panicked look</u> in my husband's eyes. He was between me and the boulder. And Elaine was about 10 and she was on the boulder with the guide.

4. James had (7) <u>gotten caught</u> under the boulder that we hit. There was a ledge that came out. When we hit it James went straight down and got caught underneath the boulder. Every time he pushed up he hit (8) <u>the top of the rock</u>. Of course he couldn't push his way out because of the current.

III. Dealing with the Accident

I spoke to James that he needs to push out to the side. James began to (9) <u>push out to</u> the side and he kind of inched his way around this boulder and then in a second or two the current took him off and got him (10) <u>out of the boulder</u>.

Scripts

Years ago we went on a family vacation to Colorado and we went whitewater rafting with my sister and her family. Everything was going along just fine. We were having a great time until we were approaching the halfway point.

And right in the middle of the river was a boulder. As we approached that halfway point we broadsided that boulder in our raft. That is the one thing that you do not want to do when you're whitewater rafting. It caused our raft to collapse. And right before we hit it though I heard just a little voice inside of my heart that said it's gonna be okay.

Well I went in the water and came up downstream and I looked back thinking my family would all be looking at me, laughing at me, that I was the one that went in the water and they didn't. But instead I saw a very panicked look in my husband's eyes. He was between me and the boulder. And Elaine was about 10 and she was on the boulder with the guide.

Robert yelled to me, "Do you see James? Do you see James?" And I couldn't see James anywhere. People on the side of the river were running up and down the river, looking to see if he might have popped up somewhere. And there was no James. Seconds were turning into an eternity. James had gotten caught under the boulder that we hit. This is a bad illustration, but it was shaped something like this. There was a ledge that came out. When we hit it James went straight down and got caught underneath the boulder. Every time he pushed up he hit the top of the rock. Of course he couldn't push his way out because of the current. Then I spoke to James that he needs to push out to the side. James began to push out to the side and he kind of inched his way around this boulder and then in a second or two the current took him off and got him out of the boulder. I'm so grateful for that. James now has our third grandson and it is truly a gift to us.

Practice

Work in groups to make a video about your experience of a disaster or an accident by using the communication skills you have learned in this unit and the outline of the above passage. You can also use some of the expressions in the sections of Listening and Watching which may help make your introduction both informative and interesting. Then upload the video onto the online learning platform for class sharing and constructive feedback.

Goal Checking:
Reflect and Evaluate

Work in groups. Reflect on and evaluate what you have learned in this unit, following the directions below.

1. Watch the videos of talking about disasters and accidents made by other groups and evaluate them according to the rubric given below.

The video is excellent because ...
• It describes the process of the disaster/accident in a detailed manner.
• The use of expressions is idiomatic and the sentences are fluent and cohesive.
• It is well designed, clearly organized and vivid in presentation.

Teaching Tips

1. Familiarize students with the purpose of this section—reflecting on and evaluating how much they have learned from this unit.
2. Have students work in groups of four and watch the videos made by other groups. Then ask students to select the best video according to the rubric given in the table.
3. Have students select the best video conforming to the rubric, watch it again and encourage students to write down as many key words and useful expressions from the best video as possible to vote for the best presenter.
4. Have students report the winner on line.

2. Select the best video conforming to the rubric above, watch it again and write down as many words and expressions of the disaster/accident as you can to vote for the best presenter.

Background of the Disaster/Accident	Occurrence of the Disaster/Accident	Dealing with the Disaster/Accident
Total Points:	Total Points:	Total Points:

Unit 5

Environmental Protection

- **Warming Up:** Think and Discuss
  Importance of Environmental Protection

- **Watching and Speaking:** Environmental Problems
  Objective: Identify and describe environmental problems

- **Listening and Speaking:** Environmental Protection
  Objective: Identify and describe environmental protection

- **Consolidating:** Give a Talk About Environmental Projects
  Objective: Talk about environmental projects

- **Goal Checking:** Reflect and Evaluate

Unit 5

Warming Up: Think and Discuss Importance of Environmental Protection

Before you start this unit, finish the following exercises with a partner.

1. Listen to the news and discuss with a partner the significance of building national parks in Qinghai-Tibet Plateau.

Keys

The region is critical to all life in China due to its rich biodiversity and Sanjiangyuan.

2. How much do you know about China's environmental protection? Do some research and share what you have found with your partner.

Words and Expressions

environmentalist *n.* a person devoted to protecting the natural environment 环保主义者

degradation *n.* the process of sth. being damaged or made worse 毁坏；恶化

biodiversity *n.* the existence of various creatures which make a balanced environment 生物多样性

Scripts

China began celebrating World Environment Day in 1985. The theme of World Environment Day in China in 2021 is "living in harmony with nature". Environmentalists, volunteers and participants from around the country are gathering in Xining to highlight the efforts to prevent, halt and reverse the degradation of the environment.

Qinghai Province, the host of the event, announced that it will speed up the building of national parks in Qinghai-Tibet Plateau, often called the "roof of the world". The region is critical to all life in China due to its rich biodiversity and Sanjiangyuan, meaning the "source of three rivers", because the province is home to the headwaters of the Yangtze, Yellow, and Lancang rivers.

Environmentalists, volunteers and enterprises have been awarded for their remarkable contributions to protecting the environment in China. Celebrities have also been invited as observers, to raise public awareness and offer suggestions.

Watching and Speaking: Environmental Problems

▶ Watching

Teaching Tips

1. Familiarize students with the purpose of this section—identifying environmental problems.
2. Call students' attention to Words and Expressions, and Notes before watching.
3. Have students pay attention to the situation of each task.
4. Have students do the tasks and check the answers.

Task 1 A Watch the video clip and decide whether each statement is T (true) or F (false).

Situation: Here is an interview about Greenland's environmental problem.

(F) **1.** Less than 80% of Greenland is made up of pure ice and has little greenery.

(T) **2.** In the central part of Greenland, the ice has a thickness of 2 miles.

(T) **3.** As the earth gets warmer, the Arctic is heating up at the doubled rate, and Greenland is warming much faster.

(F) **4.** The amount of water that's produced all across the landscape has nearly tripled in the last 15 years.

(T) **5.** The melting of Greenland helps make the large melt lakes that are forming on top of the ice sheet stunning to look at.

Words and Expressions

enormity *n.* the very great size of sth. 巨大
ice sheet a layer of ice that covers a large land for a long time 冰原；冰盖
staggering *adj.* so surprising 令人难以置信的
cascade *v.* to flow downwards in large amounts 倾泻
stack up to pile up 堆积
piercing *adj.* sharp 敏锐的
drip *n.* a small individual drop of a liquid 水滴
roar *n.* a very loud noise 轰鸣声
edge *v.* to put sth. around the edge of sth. 给……加边

Notes

Greenland island belonging to Denmark in northeastern North America (the largest island in the world) 格陵兰岛（位于北美洲东北部，是丹麦属地之一）

the Arctic the regions of the world around the North Pole 北极；北极地区

Scripts

Narrator: This is Greenland, though you will find very little greenery here. As the world's largest island, it is the home to some of the most stunning wildlife on the planet. However, more than 80% of it is made up of pure ice.

Reporter: It's only from the air that you really get a sense of the scale and the enormity of this ice sheet. And what's just staggering to imagine is that in the center of the island, this ice is 2 miles thick.

Narrator: It looks as though time has stood still for thousands of years. But this environment reflects the big changes in our world's atmosphere. As the planet gets warmer, the Arctic is heating up at the doubled rate, and Greenland, in particular, is warming even faster. Jason Box is an American climate scientist who has been coming to this remote corner of the world for more than 20 years.

Jason Box: The amount of water that's produced all across this landscape has increased like doubled in the last 50 years.

Reporter: Doubled in the last 50 years?

Jason Box: Yeah! This water cascades down thousands of feet and eventually makes its way to the bed. It's heating the bed of the ice sheet. Everything's kind of stacking up that the ice is going faster than forecast.

Reporter: And no sign of slowing down?

Jason Box: No! The melt is winning this game.

Reporter: These lakes are deceptively beautiful, because where is the white of the ice actually reflects the sunlight. The piercing blue of the lakes actively absorbs the sunlight, heating it up, and then accelerating the rate of melting.

Narrator: Everywhere you go in Greenland, you can see and hear the ice sheet melting, sometimes a drip, sometimes a roar. Surface is edged with fast flowing rivers that carry the meltwater deep down to the bed. And the more Greenland melts, the more it speeds up the melting process, making the large melt lakes that are forming on top of the ice sheet, stunning to look at but bad news for the ice.

Task ❶B Watch the video clip again and answer the following questions.

Question ❶ What is the significance of protecting the natural environment in Greenland?

As the world's largest island, Greenland is the home to some of the most stunning wildlife on the planet.

Question ❷ What is the major environmental problem in Greenland?

Its ice sheet is melting fast and shows no sign of slowing down.

Question ❸ What are the causes of the environmental problem in Greenland? And what measures can we take to handle the problem?

As the earth gets warmer, the Arctic is heating up at the doubled rate, and Greenland is warming even faster. An enormous amount of meltwater makes its way to the bed of the ice sheet and heats it. The blue of the lakes actively absorbs the sunlight, heating it up, and then accelerating the rate of melting. I believe the first thing humankind should do is to slow down the acceleration of global warming as soon as possible.

Task 2 A Watch the video clip and choose the best answer to each question you hear.

Situation: Here is a video about China's sustainable development.

(D) 1. What is the fundamental strategy for China to achieve sustainable development?
A. Establishing a commercial culture.
B. Establishing an ecological culture.
C. Establishing a commercial civilization.
D. Establishing an ecological civilization.

(B) 2. What has been considered a great success of China in global ecosystem governance?
A. The Yangtze Economic Belt.
B. The Three-North Shelter Forest Programme.
C. Returning the Grain Plots to Forestry Project.
D. The Hong Kong-Zhuhai-Macao Bridge Project.

(B) 3. What is the main target of green development according to the video?
A. To solve the problem of how man exploits nature in harmony.
B. To solve the problem of how man and nature exist in harmony.
C. To solve the problem of how to transform the country's economy.
D. To solve the problem of how to transform the country's energy.

Words and Expressions
forestry *n.* the practice of planting and taking care of trees and forests 林业
hectare *n.* a measurement of an area of land which equals 10,000 square meters 公顷
adhere *v.* to observe 遵守

Scripts

Humans and nature live together. For China, establishing an ecological civilization is a fundamental strategy in achieving sustainable development.

Every major city in China lies on a river. However, in 2013, studies revealed a shocking statistic that China's 10 biggest waterways were polluted for over half of their combined length. Of all China's rivers, the one that gives rise to the greatest concern is its mother river, the Yangtze River. The Chinese government called for a major effort to protect it and for a ban on large-scale construction along its course.

Insisting on ecology first and green development, the development path of the Yangtze Economic Belt is becoming clear. Today, the Yangtze River is generally in good condition. The water quality of the Yellow River, and two other key waterways, Heilongjiang River and Nenjiang River, has been improving.

The Three-North Shelter Forest Programme has been a great success in global ecosystem governance. Returning the Grain Plots to Forestry Project has created more than 30 million hectares of forests and grasslands in the past 20 years.

China adheres to green development, and by doing so, is helping the entire world. In spring 2019, the results of a NASA environmental study were published: from 2000 to 2017, China had been responsible for about a quarter of the new green area created worldwide. This made it the world's biggest contributor.

The main idea of green development is to solve how man and nature exist in harmony. Builders of the Hong Kong-Zhuhai-Macao Bridge have made a promise that its construction will not force the dolphins away from their natural habitat. That promise has evidently been kept.

Many of China's cities are rapidly being covered in green. China's environmental protection revolution has been transforming the country's economic and energy structure. When the ultimate goal of green development is attained, China must be a beautiful place covered with green hills and clear rivers, and filled with nostalgic memory.

Questions

1. What is the fundamental strategy for China to achieve sustainable development?
2. What has been considered a great success of China in global ecosystem governance?
3. What is the main target of green development according to the video?

Task **2 B** Watch the video clip again and answer the following questions.

Question ❶ What has China done to protect the Yangtze River? And what is the result?

The Chinese government called for a major effort to protect the Yangtze River and for a ban on large-scale construction along its course. Insisting on ecology first and green development, the development path of the Yangtze Economic Belt is becoming clear. Today, the Yangtze River is generally in good condition.

Question ❷ What contributions has China made to the global green development?

China adheres to green development, and by doing so, is helping the entire world. In spring 2019, the results of a NASA environmental study were published: from 2000 to 2017, China had been responsible for about a quarter of the new green area created worldwide, which made it the world's biggest contributor.

Question ❸ How does China handle the relationship between environmental protection and economic development? Do some research and share what you have found with your partner.

(This question is open-ended.)

▶ Speaking

Task 1 Work in groups and discuss the environmental project that impresses you the most, using some of the expressions listed below in your conversations.

What's your most impressive environmental project?	What impresses me the most is ... I am very impressed by ... As for me, ... never fails to impress.
What is the environmental problem?	In ... you can see and hear ... Greenland is warming even faster ... and its ice is melting ... Studies revealed a shocking statistic that China's ... were polluted ...
What is the result of the project?	The water quality of ... has been improving. China's environmental protection has been transforming ... The project has created ... hectares of forests and grasslands in the past ... years.

Task 2 Prepare a two-minute talk about environmental problems, covering both the causes and the solutions.

▶ Listening Skills

Learn to Make Inferences

When listening for specific information on environmental problems, pay attention to making inferences.

Making an inference means reaching a decision based on evidence we think to be true. It is a skill we use frequently in real life. For example, if a friend comes to school with a large bandage on his forehead, we infer that he/she had some kind of accident and was injured. If we wake up and see tree branches on the ground outside, we might infer that it was pretty windy last night. When we hear the words "China's establishing an ecological civilization is a fundamental strategy in achieving sustainable development", we can infer that China has made many achievements in combating her ecological problems.

Making inferences challenges the mind to work on a high level. It forces the mind to bridge the gap between the obvious and the suggested, between the stated and the unstated. Such effort requires careful listening and thinking, but rewards the listener with better and more complete understanding.

LET'S SAVE
THE WORLD TOGETHER

Practice

Listen to the following passage and pay attention to making inferences when choosing the best answer to each question.

Although commonly thought to be one of humans' feared deep-sea enemies, the octopus is generally a harmless animal that rarely bothers humans. In fact, most types of this powerful, eight armed creature are afraid of people. There have been some cases in which octopuses have attacked divers. But even these scattered attacks have not been very serious. In the mid-nineteenth century, Victor Hugo was said to have started the idea that the octopus is a vicious monster of the deep. In his *Toilers of the Sea*, he described how this devilfish eats a human being. The tale became so popular that other novelists, and later the movies, created episodes which depict a man struggling in the arms of this marine monster. And thus, the misconception of the octopus as a vicious, merciless killer was spread.

(B) 1. The listener can assume that _____.
    A. the octopus is defenseless
    B. Hugo was a popular novelist
    C. Hugo was a marine biologist
    D. the octopus is a friendly creature

(B) 2. The paragraph suggests that novelists _____.
    A. always deal with facts
    B. sometimes stretch the truth
    C. intentionally distort the truth
    D. like to write about violence

(C) 3. The speaker implies that _____.
    A. deep-sea diving is dangerous
    B. many sea creatures are harmless
    C. stories of the octopus have been exaggerated
    D. sea stories were popular in the 1800s

Listening and Speaking: Environmental Protection

▶ Listening

Teaching Tips

1. Familiarize students with the purpose of this section—understanding environmental protection.
2. Call students' attention to Words and Expressions, and Notes before listening.
3. Have students pay attention to the situation of each task.
4. Have students do the tasks and check the answers.

Task ❶ Listen to the conversation and answer the following questions.

Situation: Here is an interview about the Kekeya Green Project.

Question ❶ What's Mr. Song's first impression of Kekeya?

When he first came here, he felt so lost. It was an endless desert and there was even no grass.

Question ❷ What did Mr. Zhang's team do to combat desertification?

They built a shelter forest on the edge of the city and the aim is mainly to prevent the invasion of wind and sands. That protective forest has integrated with the city and even functions as a sightseeing attraction for urban residents.

Question ❸ How does Mr. Zhang feel about the Kekeya Green Project?

He thinks the project has brought earth-shattering changes to Aksu's environment. He is very proud and happy to see trees grow day after day and the air quality is also improved there.

Words and Expressions

desertification *n.* the process of becoming or making sth. a desert 沙漠化

integrate *v.* to combine with sth. else 使合并；成为一体

earth-shattering *adj.* very surprising or shocking 惊天动地的

Scripts

Host: In the Xinjiang Uyghur Autonomous Region, Kekeya has taken on a new look. Located at the northwestern edge of China's largest desert Takla Makan Desert, Kekeya was once known for its harsh weather conditions including frequent sandstorms. But that's now a thing in the past. The Kekeya Green Project was launched in 1986. The mission was simple: to plant more trees to fight off desert expansion. Today we invited two special guests, Mr. Song, a Kekeya forest ranger, and Mr. Zhang, the senior engineer of this project. Nice to see you, Mr. Song. You have lived in Kekeya since the tree planting project began, right? What's your first impression here?

Song: When we first came here, we felt so lost. It was an endless desert. There was even no grass. But that's over three decades ago. Forests now cover at least 80,000 hectares of Kekeya's land. Dust storms are less frequent and the area sees about 120 millimeters of rainfall per year. I'm so proud of being a part of this project.

Host: Thank you. Now, Mr. Zhang, what did your team do to combat desertification?

Zhang: We built a shelter forest on the edge of the city and the aim is mainly to prevent the invasion of wind and sands. This protective forest has integrated with the city and even functions as a sightseeing attraction for urban residents. We know China aims to increase forest coverage to over 20% by 2025.

Host: How do you feel about this project?

Zhang: The project has brought earth-shattering changes to Aksu's environment. Now we see trees grow day after day and the air quality is also improved. We are very proud and happy to see all this.

Host: Thanks for the two guests today. I believe on a grander scale, greening efforts in Kekeya will help make the place a land flowing with milk and honey.

Task 2 Listen to the passage and decide whether each statement is T (true) or F (false).

Situation: Here is a story of Gerald Ndashimye, a professional cyclist who has devoted himself to environmental protection.

(T) **1.** According to Ndashimye, cycling in the countryside is the most rewarding because of the fresh air and the green environment.

(F) **2.** Uganda has previously banned the use of single-use plastics and enforcement measures have been effected.

(T) **3.** Ndashimye's colleagues he graduated with at university were disappointed in his choosing to collect plastic waste.

(F) **4.** Ndashimye bought plastic waste recycling machines and set up his small recycling plant in a commercial area.

(T) **5.** Over the years, Ndashimye has created a team of over 70 people involved in collecting, cleaning and recycling the waste.

Words and Expressions

effect *v.* to succeed in making sth. happen 实现

commemoration *n.* a ceremony for remembering an important person or event 纪念活动

campaigner *n.* a person who leads or takes part in a campaign 运动领导者；运动参加者

meager *adj.* small in quantity and poor in quality 少量且劣质的

slum *n.* a very poor city area where the houses are in bad condition 贫民窟；棚屋区

drainage channel a passage that water can flow along 排水沟

makeshift *adj.* being used temporarily for nothing better is available 临时凑合的

Notes

Earth Hour an activity proposed by the World Wide Fund for Nature (WWF) to cope with global climate change, hoping that individuals, communities, businesses and governments turn off lights from 20:30 to 21:30 on the last Saturday of March each year, to show their support to action on climate change 地球一小时（由世界自然基金会应对全球气候变化发起的一项活动，希望个人、社区、企业和政府每年3月的最后一个星期六20:30至21:30关灯，以示支持应对气候变化的行动）

Scripts

Gerald Ndashimye has been cycling since childhood. He is now a professional cyclist. According to him, cycling in the countryside is the most rewarding because of the fresh air and the green environment. This greenery is however threatened by the poor plastic waste management in the country.

Uganda has previously banned the use of single-use plastics but enforcement measures have not been effected. During the commemoration of Earth Hour last month, environmental activists launched a campaign calling for a total ban on single-use plastics.

"Plastic waste is choking our country—polluting the air, water and soil on which both people and wildlife need to survive," the activists said in a press statement. This has forced environment protection campaigners like Ndashimye not only to create awareness about proper plastic waste disposal but also to engage in the actual cleanup.

Five years back, Ndashimye started picking up plastic waste in his community. He encouraged his colleagues to do the same so that the environment can be protected and it also protects them. The colleagues he graduated with at university were disappointed in him for his choosing to collect plastic waste instead of following his career.

Ndashimye said he does not regret the move he took, noting that step by step, with increased awareness, the environment will be protected especially against plastic waste. Using his meager resources from cycling and painting, Ndashimye bought plastic waste recycling machines. He set up his small recycling plant in a slum area in Nsambya, a suburb in the capital Kampala. "I got a place near a carpentry workshop next to a drainage channel where I built a makeshift store. I was looking at clearing my surroundings," Ndashimye said.

Over the years, he has created a team of over 70 people who are involved in the collecting of the waste, cleaning up the waste and recycling.

Task ③ Listen to the passage and fill in the blanks with the information you get.

Situation: Here is a report on the eco-friendly power plant.

Sahiwal Power Plant in Pakistan's eastern province Punjab, a major energy project under the China-Pakistan Economic Corridor, has been addressing the country's (1) <u>energy woes</u> over the years besides meeting all local and international environment protection standards.

Sprawling over hundreds of acres of land, the power plant has clusters of flowers (2) <u>blooming along</u> its driveways, lush green grass and fruit-bearing mango and guava trees which not only give an (3) <u>enchanting view</u> to the onlookers but also highlight its (4) <u>eco-friendly nature</u>.

As the World Environment Day falls on June 5, the power plant reminds that electricity generating systems across the country and the world should follow the concept of (5) <u>green development</u>.

Mr. Xu believes Sahiwal Power Plant attaches great importance to fulfillment of (6) <u>social responsibility</u> for environmental protection and it has adopted a series of strict environmental protection measures (7) <u>to minimize</u> the degree of environmental pollution.

The efforts made by the power plant in (8) <u>environmental conservation</u> provide employees with beautiful and comfortable working and living environment. Environmental protection measures of the plant have also been highly appraised by the local government.

The 1,320-megawatt coal-fired power plant has so far generated (9) <u>32.2 billion</u> kWh of electricity, significantly lessening (10) <u>power shortage</u> in the country.

Words and Expressions

woe *n.* a problem 难题

sprawl *v.* to cover a large area 伸展

cluster *n.* a group of things of the same type that grow close together 簇

guava *n.* a round, yellow, tropical fruit with pink or white flesh and hard seeds 番石榴

enchanting *adj.* charming 迷人的

glisten *v.* to shine 闪光

particulate *adj.* relating to, or in the form of tiny particles 微粒的

megawatt *n.* one million watts 兆瓦

Notes

Punjab province of northeastern Pakistan bordering on India 旁遮普省（位于巴基斯坦东北部，毗邻印度）

kWh abbreviation for kilowatt-hour 千瓦·时

Sahiwal Power Plant in Pakistan's eastern province Punjab, a major energy project under the China-Pakistan Economic Corridor, has been addressing the country's energy woes over the years besides meeting all local and international environment protection standards.

Sprawling over hundreds of acres of land, the power plant has clusters of flowers blooming along its driveways, lush green grass and fruit-bearing mango and guava trees which not only give an enchanting view to the onlookers but also highlight its eco-friendly nature. The plant's well-planned lakes glisten in the sunset with a group of ducks swimming in the water.

As the World Environment Day falls on June 5, the power plant reminds that electricity generating systems across the country and the world should follow the concept of green development.

"Sahiwal Power Plant attaches great importance to fulfillment of social responsibility for environmental protection," said Xu, Director of Corporate Culture Department of the power plant's operator.

"It has adopted a series of strict environmental protection measures to minimize the degree of environmental pollution from waste gas, wastewater, particulate matter and noise, which has enabled the plant to keep emissions well below the national standards in Pakistan and those of the World Bank," Xu added.

The efforts made by the power plant in environmental conservation provide employees with beautiful and comfortable working and living environment. Environmental protection measures of the plant have also been highly appraised by the local government. The plant has received the 13th Corporate Social Responsibility Awards and won the 16th and 17th Annual Environment Excellence Awards by the National Forum for Environment & Health of Pakistan.

The 1,320-megawatt coal-fired power plant has so far generated 32.2 billion kWh of electricity, significantly lessening power shortage in the country.

"We want to build Sahiwal Power Plant as our home, and we will certainly continue to do greening and environmental protection to make it a real 'melon and fruit garden'," Xu said.

Task 4

Listen to the passage and match the countries with the situations of garbage sorting.

Situation: Here is a talk about garbage sorting.

Finland

the UK

Japan

Korea

1. The bin will weigh the food waste and calculate the price you should pay. You have to pay for the price by scanning a barcode on the bin.

2. There are basically four types of garbage: combustible, incombustible, resources and large items. Different types of garbage are collected on different days.

3. You drop your garbage into the "smart bin" with sensors and cameras which can identify the type of the waste and place it in smaller bins.

4. You sort your waste and put it in various bins, and then it flies through these tubes to screw tanks with sensors that can alert you if those tanks are full, and a crew will come and empty it out.

■ Words and Expressions

sensor *n.* an instrument which reacts to certain physical conditions to provide information 传感器

compress *v.* to press or squeeze sth. together or into a smaller space 压紧；压缩

combustible *adj.* able to begin burning easily 易燃的；可燃的

barcode *n.* a method of representing data in a visual, machine-readable form 条形码

Since waste pollution is the common concern of humankind, some countries are making their own efforts on dealing with waste. Different countries are using different methods to sort their trash.

Like in Finland, they have built a system of Waste Transportation Tubes. You sort your waste and put it in various bins, and then it flies through these tubes to screw tanks. Those tanks have sensors on them. They can alert you if those tanks are full, and a crew will come and empty it out. They can also track where the trash comes from. It means that they know who is generating the most garbage.

A UK start-up company has invented a "smart bin" to help with garbage sorting. You just need to drop your garbage into the bin. This "smart bin" has sensors and cameras which can identify the type of the waste and place it in smaller bins. It also compresses the waste to make it occupy less space.

Well, Japan is leading the world in strict garbage sorting regulations. There are basically four types of garbage in Japan: combustible, incombustible, resources and large items. Different types of garbage are collected on different days. For example, combustible waste is typically recycled twice a week. Incombustible waste, including metals, glass, dry batteries, and so on, is collected on the third Saturday of the month. If you want to throw away larger things such as home appliances, you have to pay extra money and schedule a pickup.

Korea is using a method called "Pay for Your Trash" to encourage its people to reduce food waste. You should separate your food waste from other waste and put it into a specialized bin. The bin will weigh the food waste and calculate the price you should pay. You have to pay for the price by scanning a barcode on the bin. This can not only save food, but also help to reduce environmental pollution. It's a win-win strategy.

Speaking

Task 1 Are you interested in the environmental projects or the waste management mentioned in the Listening Section? Work in groups and discuss the topic you are most interested in, using some of the expressions listed in your conversations.

What environmental project do you know and how do you feel about it?	I know the Kekeya Green Project launched in 1986 whose mission is ... The project has brought earth-shattering changes to ... This project has been addressing ... besides meeting ...
How do you perform the waste management?	We've launched a campaign/project calling for ... We've adopted a series of strict environmental protection measures to ... We use different methods to/build a system of/adopt a win-win strategy for ...

Task 2 Prepare a two-minute talk about environmental protection, focusing on what measures you think are important. Describe the pros and cons of each of these measures.

⫸ Communication Skills

Learn to Talk About Environmental Projects

There are various ways to talk about environmental projects. One of them may include the following steps:

1. **Begin with the reasons for the environmental project.**

   - We are faced with such pollution problems as ...
   - The common concern of humankind is ...
   - This greenery is threatened by ...
   - What is choking our country now is ...

2. **Describe the goals of the environmental project.**

   - We are working on the solutions to ...
   - The goal of our project we've initiated is to ...
   - The first/second/third project is ...
   - We have launched a campaign calling for ...

3. **Specify the significance of the environmental project.**

   - This project is a great way for people to ...
   - It will allow us to learn more about ...
   - It will teach us how to ...
   - Our system will greatly reduce ...

Consolidating: Give a Talk About Environmental Projects

Teaching Tips

1. Familiarize students with the purpose of this section—practicing the communication skills.
2. Call students' attention to the expressions denoting the outline of the talk about environmental projects.
3. Have students work in groups of four, make a 5-minute video to talk about an environmental project (one student working as the photographer and the other three taking turns talking about an environmental project) and then upload the video onto the online learning platform for class sharing and constructive feedback.

Listen to the passage, fill in the blanks with the information you get, and then use them as the outline to make a video to introduce an environmental project.

I. The Eden Project

1. The goal is to create a (1) globally renowned tourism attraction.

2. The project is a great way for people to learn more about (2) green living and sustainability.

3. Visitors will learn about their own (3) environmental impact and how to reduce their (4) carbon footprints.

II. Datong Solar Power Top Runner Base

1. It is shaped like a (5) giant panda.

2. It's also one of the largest (6) solar farms in the country.

3. Its first phase was (7) recently completed.

4. The project is (8) fun and powerful.

III. China's National Carbon Market

1. It's a new, critical endeavor to attack pollution and (9) climate change.

2. It's the largest (10) carbon market in the world.

3. It is expected to cover eight (11) high-energy intensive sectors.

4. The system will greatly (12) reduce China's pollution over the next decades.

Today we're talking about some of the awesome green projects in China. Many of you might know about China's pollution problems, but you might not know about some of the solutions the government and companies are working on. So we are going to look at some of the awesome green projects in China.

The first one is the Eden Project. The goal of the project is to create a globally renowned tourism attraction in Shandong, which demonstrates sustainable construction practices and a green living. The new center will be built in Qingdao, a coastal city with nearly 9 million people between Shanghai and Beijing.

The city is backed by mountains and surrounded on three sides by the Yellow Sea. It is famous for hosting the 2008 Olympic sailing races, for having the largest bathing beach in Asia, and for its most famous export—Qingdao beer. Qingdao annually receives 63 million tourists, many of whom are from Korea and Japan. This project is a great way for people to learn more about green living and sustainability. Millions of Chinese and foreigners will visit this center each year, and learn more about their own environmental impact and how to reduce their carbon footprints.

The second one is Datong Solar Power Top Runner Base in Shanxi Province. If you like pandas, then you will like this project. This solar farm is shaped like a giant panda. It's also one of the largest solar farms in the country. China continues to lead the world in renewable energy investment. And the first phase of this solar power plant was recently completed, adding 1 GW of the estimated 5.5 GW to the electricity grid in Datong. This project is fun and powerful.

The third one is China's National Carbon Market. By setting a carbon price on the country's largest greenhouse-gas emitters, China has launched a new, critical endeavor in its effort to attack pollution and climate change. And this green initiative is the largest carbon market in the world. While the first phase of the market only covers power generation, this step will still have major climate benefits. China's power sector generates 65% of its electricity from coal and accounts for more than 3.5 gigatons of annual carbon dioxide emissions, so this new cap is almost double the European Union's carbon market, and it's 10 times the size of California's cap-and-trade systems. China's National Carbon Market is expected to expand to cover eight high-energy intensive sectors across the Chinese economy. This system will greatly reduce China's pollution over the next decades.

So these are just some of the awesome green projects in China that we find interesting. See you next time.

Practice

Work in groups to make a video about an environmental project by using the communication skills you have learned in this unit and the outline of the above passage. You can also use some of the expressions in the sections of Listening and Watching which may help make your introduction both informative and interesting. Then upload the video onto the online learning platform for class sharing and constructive feedback.

Goal Checking: Reflect and Evaluate

Work in groups. Reflect on and evaluate what you have learned in this unit, following the directions below.

1. Watch the videos of talking about environmental projects made by other groups and evaluate them according to the rubric given below.

The video is excellent because ...
• It describes the environmental project in a detailed manner.
• The use of expressions is idiomatic and the sentences are fluent and cohesive.
• It is well designed, clearly organized and vivid in presentation.

Teaching Tips

1. Familiarize students with the purpose of this section—reflecting on and evaluating how much they have learned from this unit.
2. Have students work in groups of four and watch the videos made by other groups. Then ask students to select the best video according to the rubric given in the table.
3. Have students select the best video conforming to the rubric, watch it again and encourage students to write down as many key words and useful expressions from the best video as possible to vote for the best presenter.
4. Have students report the winner on line.

2. Select the best video conforming to the rubric above, watch it again and write down as many words and expressions of the environmental project as you can to vote for the best presenter.

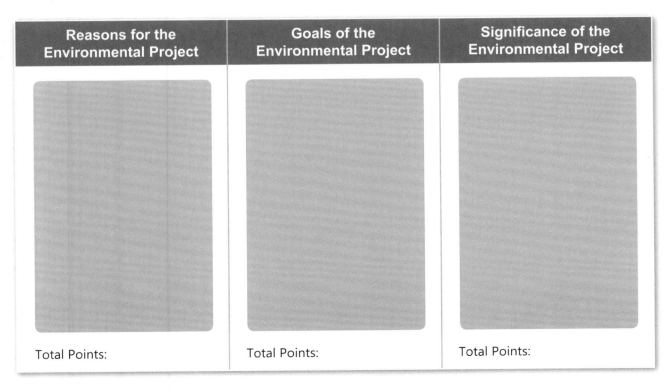

Reasons for the Environmental Project	Goals of the Environmental Project	Significance of the Environmental Project
Total Points:	Total Points:	Total Points:

Unit 6
Technology

- **Warming Up:** Think and Discuss
Role of Technology

- **Watching and Speaking:** The Importance
of Technology
Objective: Identify and describe the importance of
technology

- **Listening and Speaking:** Technological
Innovation
Objective: Identify and describe technological
innovation

- **Consolidating:** Give a Talk About Artificial
Intelligence (AI)
Objective: Talk about AI

- **Goal Checking:** Reflect and Evaluate

Teaching Tips

1. Familiarize students with the purpose of this section—arousing their interest in the topic of technology.
2. Ask if all the students have done the Warming Up exercises and check the answers in class.

Warming Up: Think and Discuss Role of Technology

Before you start this unit, finish the following exercises with a partner.

1. Listen to the news and discuss with a partner the significance of the technology utilized in the new type of relic exhibition.

Keys

The advanced technology enables this new type of relic exhibition to provide the audience with a more comprehensive experience, allowing them to feel the culture and history behind the relics through different types of digital interaction.

2. How much do you know about new Chinese technology? Do some research and share what you have found with your partner.

Words and Expressions

go viral   to spread fast like the virus 走红
holographic *adj.* connected with holograms 全息图的
refined *adj.* polite, well-educated and able to judge the quality of things 优雅的；有教养的

Notes

winding stream party   a Chinese folk custom on March 3 of the lunar calendar when people sit on both sides of a winding stream and place glasses of wine on the water which then float down, and then each person takes the glass that stops beside him and drinks the wine, which means to eliminate disasters and bad luck 曲水流觞（中国古代汉族民间的一种传统习俗，夏历的三月三日人们坐在河渠两旁，在上流放置酒杯，酒杯顺流而下，停在谁的面前，谁就取杯饮酒，意为消灾免祸）

Scripts

Recently, a special relic exhibition at the Capital Museum in Beijing went viral on Chinese social media. This digital interactive exhibition uses technology to bring relics to people—without the need for the actual relics. The beautiful digital effects are the highlight of this exhibition.

A holographic garment from the Western Han Dynasty captured the audience's attention. The actual garment, a first-grade cultural relic of China, is hung in Hunan Museum in central China's Hunan Province.

With the help of motion capture technology, the audience in Beijing can "try on" the ancient garment and make it "dance".

The ancient custom of a "winding stream party" is also a part of the exhibition, letting the audience experience the life of refined scholars from the past. If you pick up the cup floating on the digital river, a poem will emerge in front of your eyes.

"In the past, we could only see exhibits behind thick glass and learn about it through short introduction on the wall," said Ms. Hong, Director of Marketing and Public Relations Department at an Internet company.

Hong said this new type of relic exhibition provides the audience with a more comprehensive experience, allowing them to feel the culture and history behind the relics through different types of digital interaction.

The concept "technology+" has been applied in various sectors of China, and it's now helping the cultural industry to explore more possibilities.

Watching and Speaking:
The Importance of Technology

▶ Watching

Task 1 A Watch the video clip and choose the best answer to each question you hear.

Situation: Hans and Tony are having a conversation about some latest inventions worth buying.

(C) **1.** Which device can change a display into touch screen?
  A. The wearable camera.
  B. The digital fingerprint lock.
  C. The all-in-one control device.
  D. The new smartphone device.

(B) **2.** What is the storage capacity of the wearable camera?
  A. 16 gigabytes.
  B. 32 gigabytes.
  C. 64 gigabytes.
  D. 128 gigabytes.

(A) **3.** What feature makes the digital fingerprint lock suitable for hassle-free identification?
  A. It allows one to set ten fingerprints.
  B. It's low in power consumption.
  C. It's water-resistant and anti-theft.
  D. It can be carried anywhere anytime.

Words and Expressions

technophile *n.* a person who is enthusiastic about new technology 科技迷；技术爱好者

all-in-one *adj.* able to do the work of two or more things that are usually separate 几合一的

interactivity *n.* the quality that allows direct communication between the user and the machine 交互性

compatible *adj.* able to be used together 可共用的；兼容的

wearable *adj.* suitable to be worn 适于穿戴的

shock-proof *adj.* capable of absorbing shock without damage 防震的

gigabyte *n.* one thousand and twenty-four megabytes （计算机的）千兆字节

autofocus *n.* part of a camera which automatically adjusts itself so that the picture will be clear 自动聚焦装置

memorable *adj.* unforgettable 难忘的

fingerprint lock a lock that works by recognizing the fingerprint 指纹锁

biometric-enabled *adj.* able to use measurements of human features in order to identify people 具有生物识别功能的

hassle-free *adj.* not difficult 轻松的

lipstick *n.* a colored substance in the form of a stick which is put on the lips 口红；唇膏

Scripts

Hans: Hi, Tony, long time no see. I know you are a technophile. Could you please recommend some latest inventions worth buying?

Tony: Of course, Hans. I'd like to introduce to you an all-in-one control device that transforms a display into touch screen. You can connect individual smartphones and tablets for interactivity. It is compatible with any new smartphone device and brings new social media stops and other updates to your screen as well. You can enjoy playing games at home.

Hans: That sounds fun, but you know that I love going out and taking photos. Do you know any new gadget that is suitable for me?

Tony: If you're fond of taking pictures and feeling a bit uncomfortable with your mobile device, here I have a perfect option for you, a wearable camera, which gives you amazing picture quality. Its shock-proof feature allows you to use it whatever work you do. With 32-gigabyte storage capacity and autofocus mode, this device stands out from any other individual camera gadgets. It works with any social media app. This could be the best finger convenient camera device for your memorable moments.

Hans: Wow, that's cool. I'll definitely buy one. I've lost quite a few things when working out in the gym or playing soccer, you know. Do you have any suggestions?

Tony: Well, I have just the right thing for you: a digital fingerprint lock. It is a totally biometric-enabled device and can be unlocked with only your fingerprint. Its water-resistant and anti-theft features suit your all-day work. It allows you to set ten fingerprints for hassle-free identification. Only 60 grams of weight and small as a lipstick, it can be carried anywhere anytime. Its lower power consumption feature saves energy: only 2 hours of charging lasts up to 2 years. Gym, office, home or anywhere, it will stand with you as a loyal security guard.

Hans: Thanks for your recommendation! Where can I buy it? I want to place my order right away.

Questions

1. Which device can change a display into touch screen?
2. What is the storage capacity of the wearable camera?
3. What feature makes the digital fingerprint lock suitable for hassle-free identification?

Task ① B Watch the video clip again and answer the following questions.

Question ① Why does Hans ask Tony to recommend some latest inventions worth buying?

Because he knows Tony is a technophile and quite familiar with the new inventions.

Question ② What are the outstanding features of the wearable camera?

It has three outstanding features: the shock-proof feature, the autofocus mode and the capability of working with any social media app.

Question ③ Why does Tony recommend a digital fingerprint lock to Hans?

Because Hans often loses personal belongings while doing sports, and the digital fingerprint lock is a totally biometric-enabled device and can be unlocked with only the owner's fingerprint.

Task ② A Watch the video clip and fill in the blanks with the information you get.

Situation: Here is a video about the significance of technology.

Ever since the beginning of time, humans and technology (1) have lived together. Where there are humans, there's technology. Our life is always easier with technology. Through the use of spears and sharpened stones, our ancestors could take down even the largest animals. The simple technology of spears and stones made it possible for them to (2) survive and thrive.

Humans' greatest thinkers in history brought their scientific ideas and led humans to technology (3) far superior to what their previous ancestors had achieved. Owing to the developments in (4) engineering and architecture, building robust stable structures became possible. Technology (5) boosted every industry. It has changed the way people communicate and is a tool that makes our lives easier and more convenient.

The role of computers and Internet in education cannot be ignored either. The use of computers in teaching has made learning (6) <u>more interesting</u>. Technology is as important in (7) <u>the health care industry</u> as in any other. Modern discoveries of cure for diseases are made possible with the help of technology. Even (8) <u>the most dangerous diseases</u> back then are nothing to our modern-day medicines, just as planting organs and other operations are also not as difficult as before.

Even though technology (9) <u>has benefited us enormously</u>, it could do us and our environment a lot of harm too if we do not use it properly and responsibly. In good hands, technology will always be a friend to us. But in negligence and abuse, technology can also be (10) <u>our biggest foe</u>.

Words and Expressions

domesticate *v.* to cultivate 培育
fruition *n.* realization 完成；实现
negligence *n.* the failure to give sb./sth. enough care or attention 过失
foe *n.* an enemy 敌人；仇敌

Notes

Scientific Revolution the drastic change in scientific thought that took place during the 16th and 17th centuries, with a new view of nature replacing the Greek view that had dominated science for almost 2,000 years and science becoming an autonomous discipline 科学革命（发生于 16 和 17 世纪的科学思想之剧变，其特点是新自然观取代统治长达几乎两千年的希腊观，科学成为一门自主学科）

Industrial Revolution the transformation in the 18th and 19th centuries of first Britain and then other European countries and the US into industrial nations 工业革命（18 和 19 世纪首先将英国、后将其他欧洲国家和美国变为工业国家的科技革命）

Scripts

Why is technology important? Ever since the beginning of time, humans and technology have lived together. Where there are humans, there's technology. Owing to the application of technology, our way of living has evolved from hunting and gathering in the early times to planting, breeding and manufacturing at present. Our life is always easier with technology.

Through the use of spears and sharpened stones, our ancestors could take down even the largest animals. The simple technology of spears and stones made it possible for them to survive and thrive. Soon, humans began settling in areas and started cultivating and domesticating their own food. That was when agriculture was born. Gradually, new technological inventions such as ploughs and new irrigation systems made it possible for the production of vast amounts of food to feed the increasing population. With the help of technology, humans were able to cope with the ever-growing demand for food and other resources.

Many years passed and the Scientific Revolution began. Humans' greatest thinkers in history brought their scientific ideas and led humans to technology far superior to what their previous ancestors had achieved. Owing to the developments in engineering and architecture, building robust stable structures became possible. Technology boosted every industry.

Later on, the Industrial Revolution happened, and the ideas of our scientists are booked into fruition. Technology has changed the way people communicate. Communication systems have evolved from pigeons carrying messages to emails and instant messages that travel long distances in seconds, from cellular phones to smartphones which can almost do anything we've ever needed.

Technology is a tool that makes our lives easier and more convenient. The role of computers and the Internet in education cannot be ignored. The use of computers in teaching has made learning more interesting.

Technology is as important in the health care industry as in any other. Modern discoveries of cure for diseases are made possible with the help of technology. Even the most dangerous diseases back then are nothing to our modern-day medicines, just as planting organs and other operations are also not as difficult as before.

Even though technology has benefited us enormously, it could do us and our environment a lot of harm too if we do not use it properly and responsibly. In good hands, technology will always be a friend to us. But in negligence and abuse, technology can also be our biggest foe.

Task ❷ B Watch the video clip again and discuss the following questions with a partner.

Question ❶ What is the significance of technology?

Owing to the application of technology, our way of living has evolved from hunting and gathering in the early times to planting, breeding and manufacturing at present. Our life is always easier with technology, which has brought advancements in agriculture, industry, way of communication, education, etc.

Question ❷ What change has technology brought to the way people communicate?

Technology has changed the way people communicate. Communication systems have evolved from pigeons carrying messages to emails and instant messages that travel long distances in seconds, from cellular phones to smartphones which can almost do anything we've ever needed.

Question ❸ What attitude should we take toward technology?

We should take a correct attitude toward technology. On the one hand, technology has its benefits we can enjoy; on the other hand, it can be our biggest foe in negligence and abuse as it has negative effects on our environment.

⊪ Speaking

Task 1 Work in groups and discuss your knowledge, the importance and the use of technology, using some of the expressions listed below in your conversations.

What newly developed smart devices do you know or recommend?	I know a new device which is compatible with ... I know some latest inventions such as ... I want to recommend ...
Why is technology important?	This new technology allows/enables us to ... Owing to the application of technology, our way of living has ... Technology has brought advancements in ...
How should we use technology?	If we do not use technology properly and responsibly, it will ... Although technology has its benefits, we should not forget its negative effects ... In good hands, technology will ..., but in negligence and abuse, it will ...

Task 2 Prepare a two-minute talk about the importance of technology, explaining how and in what aspects technology has changed your life.

▶ Listening Skills

Learn to Identify Specific Instances

When listening for specific information on technology, pay attention to the use of specific instances in the development of a discourse. There is a very common kind of structure with the topic statement given at the beginning followed by specific instances (illustrations or examples) to make the thought clear. For example, if the statement says, "There are a lot of technological advancements in the field of education," we expect to know what the "technological advancements" are. Similarly, if the statement says, "James is the funniest technician I have seen," we naturally want to know in what respects he is so funny. This is what is called in logic reasoning from the general to the particular, and is one of the very common forms of thinking. Understanding this general-specific logical reasoning can help you follow the train of thought of the speaker and catch what he/she speaks about. In the process of listening, you can use a T-chart to help your note-taking of the topic statement and the specific instances to organize the information.

T-Chart

Topic Statement	Specific Instances

Practice

Listen to the following passage and write down its topic statement and specific instances.

Today, e-learning, as a good example of technological advancements in the field of education, is a familiar and popular term. Some of the benefits of technology in this field are:

Personalized learning experience: Learners are able to take control and manage their own learning. They set their own goals, manage the process and content of learning, and communicate with peers.

Immediate response: Most e-learning programs provide immediate feedback on learner assessments. Similarly there are features such as discussion boards and e-libraries that allow clarifications at a faster pace than in traditional classrooms.

Self-paced learning: Learners can chart courses at their own pace. This ensures higher levels of motivation both in terms of completing the course as well as in performance.

Greater access: Technological advancements have opened education to learners with learning disabilities and in remote locations.

T-Chart

Topic Statement	Specific Instances
Here are some of the benefits of technology in the field of e-learning.	1. Personalized learning experience 2. Immediate response 3. Self-paced learning 4. Greater access

Listening and Speaking: Technological Innovation

▶ Listening

Task ① Listen to the conversation and fill in the table with the information you get.

Situation: Anna and Jack are talking about some amazing inventions in the Second World Artificial Intelligence Congress.

Inventions	Functions
visual mirror	1. You can start by standing in front of the mirror and (1) <u>scanning your body</u> onto the machine. 2. You can also (2) <u>customize it</u> to make sure it looks just like you. 3. If you want to share this outfit with your friends on social media, just click (3) <u>the "share" button</u> and scan the QR code with your mobile phone.
facial recognition	1. It is displaying how technology makes (4) <u>airports smarter</u> by streamlining boarding. 2. Now we can get through the security check simply by (5) <u>scanning our faces</u>. 3. Thanks to facial recognition, not only can it (6) <u>speed up that process</u>, but it can also make our air travel more secure.
cute robot	It can (7) <u>tell stories</u>, teach kids English, recite poems, and do (8) <u>real-time voice translation</u>, working presumably as a classmate, a friend and (9) <u>a teacher</u>.

Words and Expressions

marvelous *adj.* lovely 令人愉快的   **terrific** *adj.* extremely good 绝妙的

virtual *adj.* made to appear to exist by the use of computer software 虚拟的

customize *v.* to make or change sth. to suit the needs of the owner 订制

outfit *n.* a set of equipment that you need for a particular purpose 全套装备

converge *v.* to meet or join at a particular place 交叉

streamline *v.* to make a system more efficient by removing its unnecessary parts 提高……的效率

real-time *adj.* of or relating to computer systems that update information at the same rate they receive information （计算机数据处理）实时的

presumably *adv.* probably 很可能

Scripts

Anna: Jack, I'm so excited to be here. I still can't believe that we really made it to the Second World Artificial Intelligence Congress in Tianjin. It seems like we are walking into a marvelous wonderland! I can't believe my eyes!

Jack: Anna, just relax and take it easy. I've already dug some information about this congress. Today I'll be your guide to show you some amazing inventions.

Anna: That's terrific! Hey, there are many people taking pictures in front of a big mirror. Let's go and check it out.

Jack: This is a virtual mirror. You can start by standing in front of the mirror and scanning your body onto the machine. You can also customize it to make sure it looks just like you. If you want to share this outfit with your friends on social media, just click the "share" button and scan the QR code with your mobile phone.

Anna: Smart mirrors like this converging online and offline are bringing us a new lifestyle. I want to take this mirror home. I love it! Look, that looks like a security gate. What are they doing?

Jack: That is facial recognition technology. It is displaying how technology makes airports smarter by streamlining boarding. Long queues at the airport can make us feel a bit anxious. Now we can get through the security check simply by scanning our faces. Thanks to facial recognition, not only can it speed up that process, but it can also make our air travel more secure.

Anna: Oh, I remember that in high-speed railway stations, it indeed saved us a lot of time. Wow, look at this cute robot. What can it do?

Jack: It can tell stories, teach kids English, recite poems, and do real-time voice translation, working presumably as a classmate, a friend and a teacher.

Anna: It's really beneficial to early childhood education. Let's go and explore more together.

Task ❷ Listen to the passage and choose the best answer to each question you hear.

Situation: Here is a report about 5G technology being implemented in the coal mine in Shanxi Province.

(B) **1.** How did workers call for vehicles in the past?
A. Through mobile phones.
B. Through wired telephones.
C. Through wireless telephones.
D. Through video calls.

(A) **2.** Which of the following is NOT the change that 5G brings to the coal mine?
A. Sending signals from the ground above.
B. Allowing for one-click vehicle hailing.
C. Intelligent patrolling by robots.
D. Smooth video calls with ground staff.

(C) **3.** What's the impact of 5G on Shanxi's energy development?
A. It speeds up development in the province's power generation.
B. It speeds up coal production capacity in the whole province.
C. It speeds up development in clean energy and new energy.
D. It speeds up promotion of new energy research institutes.

Words and Expressions

hail *v.* to signal to a vehicle in order to make it stop 发信号或示意（使车辆等停下）
patrol *v.* to go around an area regularly to check that there is no trouble 巡查；巡逻
supervision *n.* management 监管
implement *v.* to do 实施
photovoltaic *adj.* using sunlight to produce electricity 光电的；光伏的

In a coal mine 500 meters underground, Chen, a technician with Tashan Coal Mine, located in the city of Datong, North China's Shanxi Province, holds a 5G mobile phone, opens an app and taps the screen to hail a vehicle. In less than a minute, a rubber-tyred vehicle approached.

"In the past, workers had to call for vehicles through wired telephones and wait for word from the ground above," said Chen.

The introduction of the 5G network in this coal mine has changed things, with services allowing for one-click vehicle hailing, intelligent patrolling by robots and smooth video calls with ground staff.

As one of the first pilot smart coal mines in China, Tashan Coal Mine widely utilizes 5G technology and has realized 24-hour supervision. "Technology has changed the traditional way of development, and the future of coal mines is green and efficient," Chen said.

Shanxi is one of China's coal-rich provinces. In recent years, the province has continued to deepen the supply-side structural reform of the energy industry. During the 13th Five-Year Plan period (2016–2020), it eliminated 157 million tons of excess coal production capacity, and 55 coal mines in the province have adopted green mining practices.

At present, 5G technology has been implemented in some coal mines in Shanxi, reducing work intensity, and improving safety and production. Meanwhile, a number of leading scientific research institutes are on the rise in Shanxi. For example, a national laboratory is under construction to realize the green utilization of coal, in addition to eight new research institutes.

Inspired by its success in the coal sector, Shanxi is speeding up development in clean energy and new energy, such as photovoltaic and wind power.

By the end of 2020, the province's installed power generation capacity had exceeded 100 million kilowatts, with new energy accounting for more than 30 percent.

"New energy vehicles are green, environmentally friendly and low-carbon. It will be a trend in the development of the automobile industry in the future," Yuan said.

Questions

1. How did workers call for vehicles in the past?
2. Which of the following is NOT the change that 5G brings to the coal mine?
3. What's the impact of 5G on Shanxi's energy development?

Task 3

Listen to the passage and finish the table with the names of different jobs listed in the following box.

Situation: Here is a report on how AI will change the future job market.

cashier	mining	journalist
firefighting	courier services	writing software
telemarketer	bank teller	deep-sea oil drilling
pizza delivery	construction working	repairing and maintaining robots
truck driver	receptionist	developing new and better systems

The ordinary jobs to be taken over by AI	The dangerous jobs to be taken over by AI	The new jobs to be opened up
cashier receptionist telemarketer bank teller truck driver courier services pizza delivery journalist	firefighting mining deep-sea oil drilling construction working	writing software repairing and maintaining robots developing new and better systems

Words and Expressions

algorithm *n.* a series of mathematical steps which gives the answer to a kind of problem 算法

obsolete *adj.* outdated 过时的

telemarketer *n.* a salesperson who telephones people to persuade them to buy some products or services 电话营销员

bank teller a person whose job is to receive and pay out money in a bank 银行柜员

drone *n.* an aircraft without a pilot, controlled from the ground 无人驾驶飞机

courier *n.* a person or company whose job is to take packages or important papers somewhere （递送包裹或重要文件的）信使，通讯员，专递公司

accommodate *v.* to adapt 适应

mortality rate death rate 死亡率

hazardous *adj.* dangerous 危险的

In the last decade, artificial intelligence has gone from a science fiction dream to a critical part of our everyday life. We use AI systems to interact with our phones. Smart cars interpret and analyze their surroundings to intelligently drive themselves. Online shopping platforms monitor our browsing habits and intelligently serve up products they think we'd like to buy. Artificially intelligent algorithms are here, but this is only the beginning, because in the future AI is going to change everything.

Now, let's take a look at some of the most groundbreaking developments we expect to see in the very near future and whether that's a step forward or backward for society.

First and foremost, AI systems are already prime to take over thousands if not millions of jobs. Any job that consists of a human taking down information from other humans and inputting it into a system is likely to go obsolete. So cashiers, receptionists, telemarketers and bank tellers are all on their way out. As self-driving cars, self-operating drones get more complex, we will also lose jobs like truck drivers, courier services, even pizza delivery. Factories are also becoming fully automated. So our car washes and movie theaters, even my job as a journalist, are threatened by rapidly improving algorithms that can gather information and deliver it faster and more accurately.

But as society changes to accommodate in an all-machines-service world, it will also open up new jobs for the next generation: writing software, repairing and maintaining robots and developing new and better systems. Most notably, machines are also prime to take over dangerous jobs: firefighting, mining, deep-sea oil drilling, construction working and other careers with high mortality rates will be replaced by machines that won't get sick or hurt. We don't know what an all AI workforce will look like yet, but many economists believe that the world might be a brighter and more rewarding place with machines taking over the duller and hazardous jobs.

Task 4 Listen to the passage and answer the following questions.

Situation: Here is a talk about the 5G era.

Question 1 What progress has China achieved in the new technological era?

China has achieved remarkable progress in 5G patents, standards, evaluation licenses and network deployments.

Question 2 What's the key to next generation technology revolution?

Improving independent innovation ability and gaining innovative development initiative is the key.

Question 3 What benefits can we get from 5G applications?

5G applications help expand communication from person-to-person, to person-to-thing, thing-to-thing and beyond. It starts the ubiquitous interconnection of all things, human-machine interaction, and the change led by intelligence.

▌ *Words and Expressions*

patent *n.* an official right to be the only person to make, use or sell a product or an invention 专利

deployment *n.* the distribution of equipment in preparation for work 部署

underpin *v.* to support or strengthen 巩固；支撑

innovative *adj.* creative 创新的

ubiquitous *adj.* very common 无所不在的

at the forefront   in an important or leading position 处于最前列

Everyone has been talking about 5G since 2019. 5G is an "across generation" technology. On June 6, 2019, China's Ministry of Industry and Information Technology issued four commercial licenses for 5G. The country has officially entered a new technological era, racing along the 5G track. China has achieved remarkable progress in 5G patents, standards, evaluation licenses and network deployments. For example, its 5G patents account for over 30% of the world's total, ranking the first. By the end of 2019, more than 130,000 5G base stations had been built nationwide. In 7 years, the existing 5.5 million 4G base stations will be upgraded to 5G and the combined total of 5G base stations will reach 6 million in China by 2027.

Meanwhile, people start to enjoy more 5G applications in daily life: folding-screen phones, faster check-in at railway stations and higher quality TV shows. A worldwide competition for 5G market share is coming. The US, Switzerland and others have all launched 5G commercial services. It is the network that will underpin the entire next generation technology revolution.

So improving independent innovation ability and gaining innovative development initiative is the key. 5G applications help expand communication from person-to-person, to person-to-thing, thing-to-thing and beyond. It starts the ubiquitous interconnection of all things, human-machine interaction, and the change led by intelligence. 5G will be at the forefront of a new round of technological and industrial revolution. The possibilities are endless, but most people associate 5G with one word: fast. Speed and new technologies are important, but 5G is about much more. The 5G era has come. The vision of the Internet of everything is being realized. But new services, new frameworks and new technologies will also post new challenges to big data security and users' privacy protection.

Speaking

Teaching Tips

1. Familiarize students with the purpose of this section—reflecting on and evaluating what they have learned from the Listening Section.
2. Have students do the tasks and check the answers.

Task 1 Are you interested in the technological innovation mentioned in the Listening Section? Work in groups and discuss the one you like best in detail, using some of the expressions listed below in your conversations.

Of the technologies mentioned in the Listening Section, which interests you the most and why?	Of the technologies, I'm really interested in ..., because ... Among the technologies, I have a great interest in ... With a strong passion for ..., I'm really attracted by ...
What benefits can we get from the new technology?	The new technology can bring/save ... The new technology has changed/reduced/improved ... The new technology is really beneficial to ...
What do you think of the future of our society with new technologies?	Our society will change/open up new jobs for ... Dangerous jobs will be taken over by ... Careers with high mortality rates will be replaced by ...

Task 2 Prepare a two-minute talk about a technological innovation you are interested in, describing its development, features as well as its impact on your life.

▶ Communication Skills

Learn to Talk About Artificial Intelligence (AI)

There are various ways to talk about AI. One of them may include the following steps:

1. **Describe the importance of AI.**

   - AI can fuel such technologies as ...
   - AI has the potential to ...
   - AI has changed the traditional way of ...
   - We use AI systems to ...

2. **Describe the blueprint for AI.**

   - We aim to create ...
   - In ... our AI evolution has reached ...
   - Our government has announced its ambitious plan to ...
   - Our plan is broken up into three benchmarks ...

3. **Describe the conditions for the development of AI.**

   - We have invested a lot in/poured a large sum of money into ...
   - Our rise in AI can boil down to ...
   - We have some favorable conditions for ...
   - We have more advantages in ...

Consolidating: Give a Talk About Artificial Intelligence (AI)

Teaching Tips

1. Familiarize students with the purpose of this section—practicing the communication skills.
2. Call students' attention to the expressions denoting the outline of the talk about AI.
3. Have students work in groups of four, make a 5-minute video to talk about AI (one student working as the photographer and the other three as participants taking turns talking about AI) and then upload the video onto the online learning platform for class sharing and constructive feedback.

Listen to the passage, fill in the blanks with the information you get, and then use them as the outline to make a video to introduce AI.

I. **The Importance of AI**

1. Some of the technologies that AI is fueling: cars that drive themselves, (1) facial recognition, detecting cancer potentially better than a doctor;

2. The potential to (2) add trillions of dollars to a nation's GDP.

II. **The Blueprint for China's AI**

1. To keep pace with (3) AI technologies by 2020;

2. To achieve (4) AI breakthroughs by 2025;

3. To be (5) the world leader in AI by 2030.

III. **The Conditions for the Development of China's AI**

1. The large investment: in 2017, (6) Chinese venture capital investors poured record sums of money into AI, (7) making up 48% of all AI venture funding globally;

2. The large population: China has (8) large IT population which is around 1.4 billion.

Cars that drive themselves, facial recognition, detecting cancer potentially better than a doctor—these are just some of the technologies that artificial intelligence (AI) is fueling. With the potential to add trillions of dollars to a nation's GDP, the race to become an AI super power is on.

China's rise in AI is relatively recent. In May, 2017, China's AI evolution reached a symbolic moment. Some people even called it a wake-up call. Weiqi is a game that's been played in China for thousands of years and is said to be the world's most complex game. Ke Jie, a 19-year-old Chinese boy, is known to be the world's best player. He was challenged to compete against AlphaGo designed by the parent company of Google. He lost. Less than two months after the defeat, China announced its ambitious plans to build up artificial intelligence capabilities. As part of its existing 2025 plan, it aims to create a next generation artificial intelligence development plan.

The plan is broken up into three benchmarks: to keep pace with AI technologies by 2020, to achieve AI breakthroughs by 2025, and to actually be the world leader in AI by 2030. A report delivered at the 19th National Congress of the Communist Party of China said, "We will work faster to build China into a manufacturer of quality and develop advanced manufacturing, promote further integration of the Internet, big data, and artificial intelligence with the real economy." To get there, it's investing a lot. In 2017, Chinese venture capital investors poured record sums of money into AI, making up 48% of all AI venture funding globally. Chinese startups raised 4.9 billion dollars while their US counterparts raised 4.4 billion.

In addition to the large investment, China's rise in AI can also boil down to her large IT population which is at around 1.4 billion. Taking all these into account, we can say China's rise in AI is spectacular in deed.

Practice

Work in groups to make a video about AI by using the communication skills you have learned in this unit and the outline of the above passage. You can also use some of the expressions in the sections of Listening and Watching which may help make your introduction both informative and interesting. Then upload the video onto the online learning platform for class sharing and constructive feedback.

Goal Checking: Reflect and Evaluate

Work in groups. Reflect on and evaluate what you have learned in this unit, following the directions below.

1. Watch the videos of talking about artificial intelligence made by other groups and evaluate them according to the rubric given below.

The video is excellent because ...

- It describes AI in a detailed manner.

- The use of expressions is idiomatic and the sentences are fluent and cohesive.

- It is well designed, clearly organized and vivid in presentation.

Teaching Tips

1. Familiarize students with the purpose of this section—reflecting on and evaluating how much they have learned from this unit.

2. Have students work in groups of four and watch the videos made by other groups. Then ask students to select the best video according to the rubric given in the table.

3. Have students select the best video conforming to the rubric, watch it again and encourage students to write down as many key words and useful expressions from the best video as possible to vote for the best presenter.

4. Have students report the winner on line.

2. Select the best video conforming to the rubric above, watch it again and write down as many words and expressions of AI as you can to vote for the best presenter.

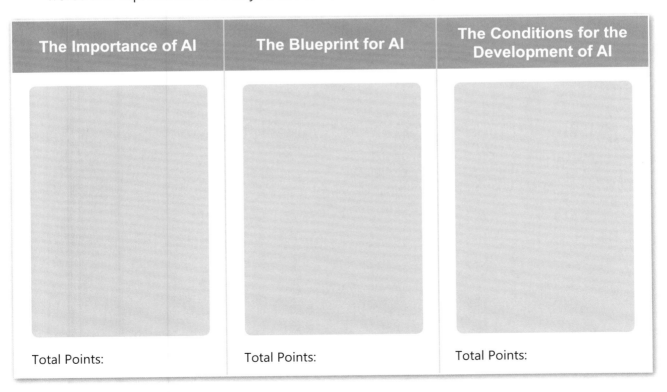

The Importance of AI	The Blueprint for AI	The Conditions for the Development of AI
Total Points:	Total Points:	Total Points:

Unit 7
21st Century Skills

- **Warming Up:** Think and Discuss
  Role of 21st Century Skills

- **Watching and Speaking:** The Necessity
  for 21st Century Skills
  Objective: Identify and describe the necessity for 21st
  century skills

- **Listening and Speaking:** The Types of
  21st Century Skills
  Objective: Identify and describe the types of 21st
  century skills

- **Consolidating:** Give a Talk About 21st
  Century Skills/Competencies
  Objective: Talk about 21st century skills/competencies

- **Goal Checking:** Reflect and Evaluate

Teaching Tips

1. Familiarize students with the purpose of this section—arousing their interest in the topic of 21st century skills.
2. Ask if all the students have done the Warming Up exercises and check the answers in class.

Warming Up: Think and Discuss Role of 21st Century Skills

Before you start this unit, finish the following exercises with a partner.

1. Listen to the news and discuss with a partner why 21st century skills have recently taken a more central role in policy discussions.

Keys

21st century skills or 21st century competencies have recently taken a more central role in policy discussions, because they are seen as critical components of college and career readiness.

2. How much do you know about 21st century skills? Do some research and share what you have found with your partner.

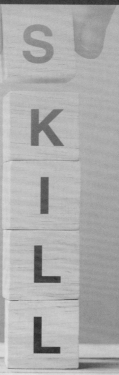

Words and Expressions

adaptability *n.* the ability to change to fit changed circumstances 适应性

confluence *n.* the fact of two or more things becoming one 汇合

perception *n.* the way that you notice things, esp. with the senses 感知

disposition *n.* the natural qualities of a person's character 性格

pedagogy *n.* the study of teaching methods 教学法

Scripts

Public school systems are expected to promote a wide variety of skills and accomplishments in their students, including both academic achievement and the development of broader competencies, such as creativity, adaptability, and global awareness. The latter outcomes, which are often referred to as 21st century skills or 21st century competencies have recently taken a more central role in policy discussions, because they are seen as critical components of college and career readiness. This growing emphasis on outcomes beyond simple academic content knowledge is the result of a confluence of factors, including perceptions among some business and government leaders that globalization, technology, migration, international competition and changing markets require a greater emphasis on these outcomes than was required in the past.

As a result, school systems are facing increasing pressure to produce graduates with this range of competencies which include knowledge, skills, attitudes, and dispositions, a demand that generates challenges in terms of pedagogy and assessment.

Watching and Speaking: The Necessity for 21st Century Skills

▶ Watching

Teaching Tips

1. Familiarize students with the purpose of this section—identifying the necessity for 21st century skills.
2. Call students' attention to Words and Expressions before watching.
3. Have students pay attention to the situation of each task.
4. Have students do the tasks and check the answers.

Task 1 A Watch the video clip and choose the best answer to each question you hear.

Situation: A reporter and a school principal are having a conversation about 21st century skills taught in the school.

(B) 1. Apart from some basic courses, what are taught to children in the school?
A. Language skills.
B. 21st century skills.
C. Neither A nor B.
D. Both A and B.

(A) 2. How often is the full meeting held among the teaching team members?
A. At least once a week.
B. At least twice a week.
C. At least once a month.
D. At least twice a month.

(C) 3. Which system is utilized to record each student's behavior through his/her academic career?
A. A full-time social system.
B. A system of common core.
C. A system of documentation.
D. A system of code of conduct.

Words and Expressions

leadership *n.* the ability to be a leader or the qualities a good leader should have 领导才能

collaboration *n.* the act of working with others to create or produce sth. 合作

common core basic courses 基础课

liaison *n.* a person whose job is to encourage co-operation and the exchange of information 联络员

documentation *n.* the act of recording sth. in a document 文献记录

Scripts

Reporter: What do you teach the children in your school apart from some basic courses?

Principal: We support children with their personal, social and emotional development. On top of that, we teach 21st century skills.

Reporter: So what are 21st century skills?

Principal: Well, we talk about leadership, creativity, critical thinking, problem solving, collaboration, communication skills and more. Learning these skills is now more important than ever.

Reporter: How are teaching and learning these skills—critical thinking, creative thinking, collaborating and communicating—implemented in your school and classroom?

Principal: The students used to be OK with answering the question right, but nowadays they must demonstrate how they work out the answer and why they think the answer is right. Critical thinking skills are emphasized in curriculum now more than ever with the implementation of common core.

Reporter: How is the teaching of 21st century skills being implemented in the schools of your district now?

Principal: Our district is assigning creativity liaisons to be partnered with an institute in Greenwood to develop creative learning in each school. Collaboration and communication are a huge part of teaching nowadays. At least one full meeting is held every week among the teaching team members of every grade in order to share new ideas or strategies. And collaborated learning is taught in the classroom as well.

Reporter: How about media and technology literacy?

Principal: We've had a very basic level of media and technology literacy now. But we need to do more in this aspect so as to implement technology and media literacy classwork better.

Reporter: Last question! How are life skills taught in your school?

Principal: With common core funding, our school now has a full-time social worker, a regular psychologist, and a code of conduct—"Be respectful, be responsible, be safe, and be a scholar." We also implement a documentation system on student behavior which follows every student through his/her academic career.

Reporter: Thank you so much for your time!

Principal: You're welcome!

Questions

1. Apart from some basic courses, what are taught to children in the school?

2. How often is the full meeting held among the teaching team members?

3. Which system is utilized to record each student's behavior through his/her academic career?

Task ① B Watch the video clip again and answer the following questions.

Question ① What do 21st century skills include?

21st century skills include leadership, creativity, critical thinking, problem solving, collaboration, communication skills and more.

Question ② How is the teaching of 21st century skills implemented in the school now?

Their district is assigning creativity liaisons to be partnered with an institute in Greenwood to develop creative learning in each school. At least one full meeting is held every week among the teaching team members of every grade in order to share new ideas or strategies.

Question ③ How does the school principal think about technology and media literacy in the school?

According to the school principal, the school has had a very basic level of media and technology literacy now. But they want to do more in this aspect so as to implement technology and media literacy classwork better.

Task 2 A Watch the video clip and finish the table with the names of different skills listed in the following box.

Situation: Here is a video about the classification of 21st century skills.

communication	collaboration	creativity	flexibility
initiative	leadership	information literacy	social skills
media literacy	technology literacy	critical thinking	productivity

21st Century Skills		
Learning Skills	**Literacy Skills**	**Life Skills**
creativity critical thinking collaboration communication	information literacy media literacy technology literacy	flexibility leadership initiative productivity social skills

Words and Expressions

server *n.* part of a computer network which does a particular task 服务器

savvy *adj.* having practical knowledge and understanding of sth. 有见识的

well-rounded *adj.* having a variety of abilities and a fully developed personality 全面发展的

discern *v.* to identify 识别

Have you heard of the term "21st century skills" lately? Does it seem weird that nobody ever takes the time to really explain what that means? I'm Mark, an education reporter, and today I'm going to answer the question. What are 21st century skills? 21st century skills refer to 12 abilities that students need to succeed in the age of the Internet. These 12 abilities are grouped into three different categories.

I'll start by talking about learning skills, the first category. Learning skills, also called the 4Cs, help students adapt and improve in the workplace. They include creativity, critical thinking, collaboration and communication. All of them are skills that students can use later in life to adapt to any situation that they can encounter on the job.

Our next category is called literacy skills which are of three kinds. And they all deal with reading and understanding information, especially the information students find online. The first skill is information literacy. This means when students read something online they understand what that is actually saying, whether it's a newspaper article or a blog from a source that they just find that day. The second skill is media literacy that means understanding the sources that publish that information and whether those sources are reliable. Finally, there's technology literacy. Technology literacy means understanding the machinery, servers and computers. These three skills help students become savvy. And they also help students become challenging independent thinkers in the age of the Internet.

The third category of skills is called life skills. It's also sometimes called FLIPS, which includes flexibility, leadership, initiative, productivity and social skills. These skills are the ones that students can use as they go through their lives, dealing with technology in a variety of different ways, whether that be their personal smartphone or their workplace computer. Students are bound to use all of these skills in their personal lives and their professional lives.

All of these skills help students for decades to come. When students equip themselves with these 21st century skills, they'll become well-rounded people who are able to discern accurate information in an age when there is so much data out there for them to process.

Task ②B Watch the video clip again and discuss the following questions with a partner.

Question ① Why are learning skills important to students?

Learning skills help students adapt and improve in the workplace. All of them are skills that students

can use later in life to adapt to any situation that they can encounter on the job.

Question ② What does information literacy mean to students?

It means when students read something online they understand what that is actually saying,

whether it's a newspaper article or a blog from a source that they just find that day.

Question ③ What is the significance of 21st century skills?

All of these skills help students for decades to come. When students equip themselves with

these 21st century skills, they'll become well-rounded people who are able to discern accurate

information in an age when there is so much data out there for them to process.

⠿ Speaking

Teaching Tips

1. Familiarize students with the purpose of this section—reflecting on and evaluating what they have learned from the Watching Section.
2. Have students do the tasks and check the answers.

Task  Work in groups and discuss the need of 21st century skills in details, using some of the expressions listed below in your conversations.

What are 21st century skills?	21st century skills include ... 21st century skills refer to ... 21st century skills can be grouped into ... Public school systems are expected to promote a wide variety of skills including ...
How does your school teach 21st century skills?	Our school now has developed .... Besides, we also support students with ... At present, our curriculum includes ... Teachers demonstrate more enthusiasm in ...
Why are 21st century skills so important?	Because they are seen as ... The growing emphasis on 21st century skills is the result of ... All of these skills can help ... With 21st century skills, students will become well-rounded people who ...

Task ❷ Prepare a two-minute talk about the necessity for 21st century skills, explaining why they are important to our daily life and what problems they may create if utilized inappropriately.

⫸ Listening Skills

Teaching Tips

1. Familiarize students with the purpose of this section—learning to identify logical reasoning.
2. Have students do the listening exercises and check the answers.

Learn to Identify Logical Reasoning

When listening for specific information on skills for the 21st century, pay attention to types of logical reasoning used in the text. One often-used logical reasoning is deduction, which gives the premises first and then gives the conclusion that is based on and supported by the premises, i.e., if the premises are true, then the conclusion must be true. For example,

21st century skills are very important.

Critical thinking is a 21st century skill.

So critical thinking is very important.

During the listening process, you can also use a T-chart to take notes of both the premises and the conclusion.

T-Chart

Premise 1	21st century skills are very important.
Premise 2	Critical thinking is a 21st century skill.
Conclusion	So critical thinking is very important.

Practice

Listen to the following passage and write down the premises and the conclusion in the T-chart while listening.

Learning new skills opens doors. When you learn a new language, doors open for you to work in different sectors of our country that need dual-language speakers, not to mention overseas. When you learn how to program, you stand a better chance of serving the people. When you learn how to play an instrument, you open up a new stream that makes others happy. When you learn how to design websites, write essays, or perform virtual secretary skills, you become eligible for part-time freelance opportunities to do more for society. In a nutshell, whichever new skill you acquire, a new door of opportunity will always open for you.

T-Chart

Premise 1	Learning new skills opens doors.
Premise 2	When you learn a new language, doors open for you to work in different sectors of our country that need dual-language speakers, not to mention overseas.
Premise 3	When you learn how to program, you stand a better chance of serving the people.
Premise 4	When you learn how to play an instrument, you open up a new stream that makes others happy.
Premise 5	When you learn how to design websites, write essays, or perform virtual secretary skills, you become eligible for part-time freelance opportunities to do more for society.
Conclusion	In a nutshell, whichever new skill you acquire, a new door of opportunity will always open for you.

Listening and Speaking: The Types of 21st Century Skills

▸ Listening

Task 1   Listen to the passage, fill in the blanks with what you hear and match the terms with the situations of multipotentiality.

Situation: Here is a conversation about the importance of multipotentiality.

idea synthesis

adaptability

rapid learning

1. He is sometimes a video director, sometimes a web designer, sometimes a (1) <u>website consultant</u>, sometimes a teacher, and sometimes an actor. He's valuable because he can (2) <u>take on various roles</u>, depending on (3) <u>his clients' needs</u>.

2. When they become interested in something, they can start learning for they're less afraid of (4) <u>trying new things</u> and stepping out of (5) <u>their comfort zones</u>. They bring everything they've learned to (6) <u>every new area they pursue</u>, so they're rarely (7) <u>starting from scratch</u>.

3. They drew from their shared interests in cartography, (8) <u>data visualization</u>, travel, mathematics and design, when they founded a company that creates custom (9) <u>geographically-inspired jewelry</u>. They came up with this unique idea because of their (10) <u>eclectic mix of skills and experiences</u>.

Words and Expressions

multipotentialite *n.* a person with many qualities capable of being developed 多项潜能者

hold water to be sound, valid, capable of standing up to testing 有理

affliction *n.* sth. which causes physical or mental suffering 折磨

cartography *n.* the art of drawing or making maps 制图学

data visualization the act or an instance of visualizing data 数据可视化

eclectic *adj.* choosing from or using a wide variety 不拘一格的

start from scratch to begin at the beginning 从头做起

morph *v.* to change, or make sb./sth. change 改变

Scripts

A: What will you do if there are a lot of different subjects you're curious about, and many different things you want to do?

B: Do you mean a multipotentialite with many interests and creative pursuits?

A: Right!

B: I have to say I find it sort of fitting that as a community, we cannot agree on a single identity.

A: If that holds water, then how to understand the old saying "Grasp all, lose all"?

B: It's easy to see your multipotentiality as a limitation or an affliction that you need to overcome. But what I've learned through speaking with people and writing about these ideas on my website is that there are some tremendous strengths.

A: What are the strengths?

B: I think there are three strengths. The first one is idea synthesis which means combining two or more fields and creating something new at the intersection. Two friends of mine drew from their shared interests in cartography, data visualization, travel, mathematics and design, when they founded a company that creates custom jewelry with local color. They came up with this unique idea because of their eclectic mix of skills and experiences.

A: What about the second one?

B: The second is rapid learning. When multipotentialites become interested in something, they can start learning, because they've been beginners so many times in the past, and this means that they're less afraid of trying new things and stepping out of their comfort zones. What's more, many skills are transferable across disciplines, and multipotentialites bring everything they've learned to every new area they pursue, so they're rarely starting from scratch.

A: I guess the third strength is adaptability.

B: Quite right! Adaptability is the ability to morph into whatever you need to be in a given situation. My brother is sometimes a video director, sometimes a web designer, sometimes a website consultant, sometimes a teacher, and sometimes, apparently, an actor. He's valuable because he can take on various roles, depending on his clients' needs. Such adaptability is identified as the single most important skill to develop in order to thrive in the 21st century.

A: Great! What you say is convincing.

Task 2 Listen to the passage and choose the best answer to each question you hear.

Situation: Here is a passage about critical thinking.

(C) **1.** What is critical thinking mainly about?

A. Asking the right questions that help to draw conclusions.

B. Answering the right questions that help to draw conclusions.

C. Asking questions helpful to assess the claim, reasoning and evidence.

D. Answering questions helpful to assess the claim, reasoning and evidence.

(B) **2.** Which action is NOT included in the process of critical thinking?

A. Discovering the key points.

B. Finding flaws in the case analysis.

C. Analyzing the information sources.

D. Weighing various types of evidence.

(D) **3.** How does thinking critically help people feel confident in their own opinions and conclusions?

A. By helping them share the views of a close friend.

B. By helping them take a public stand for themselves.

C. By helping them follow certain beliefs that just feel right.

D. By helping them become creative, reflective and adaptable.

▌Words and Expressions

merit *n.* strength 优点

consequence *n.* importance 重要性

flaw *n.* fault 缺陷

reflective *adj.* thoughtful 深思的

sway *v.* to influence 影响

▌Notes

Sherlock Holmes   a fictional private detective created by British author Sir Arthur Conan Doyle 夏洛克·福尔摩斯（英国小说家柯南·道尔塑造的著名侦探）

Critical

Thinking

Scripts

When you are given the facts you require, you will memorize the facts and use them to serve your short-term goals of passing tests and graduating to a higher class. When you develop critical thinking skills, you will be able to find the necessary information by yourself, and you'll be able to evaluate the merits and consequences of that information and utilize it to solve any problems at hand.

Critical thinking is all about asking the right questions that help you assess both the claim and the reasoning and evidence used to support it. Building such skills and applying them in your life make it easier for you to assess arguments, evaluate evidence, and respond and act thoughtfully. With critical analysis of facts to form your judgment, you can stay engaged in different situations in a sensible way.

Critical thinking involves stepping back from a situation to enable you to see diverse angles before making judgments or taking actions. It means identifying the key points, analyzing the sources of information, weighing different types of evidence, just as Sherlock Holmes did in a case analysis, and putting all together into your own independent thought to form a well-informed, well-thought-out position of your own.

One important thing to realize is that critical thinking isn't about being critical. It's about much more than just finding flaws in other people's claims. Critical thinking means being creative, reflective and adaptable in evaluating the evidence to decide for yourself what is accurate and what is relevant. In most cases, you may ask yourself, "Do I have sufficient information to make a judgment on this topic?" Thinking critically means taking a stand for yourself. It may be difficult not to be swayed by the views of a close friend or certain beliefs that just feel right, but learning how to use the higher thinking skills can help you feel much more confident in your own opinions and conclusions.

By learning to think critically, you'll find you're becoming a clearer thinker, and then you can learn better and aim higher.

Questions

1. What is critical thinking mainly about?

2. Which action is NOT included in the process of critical thinking?

3. How does thinking critically help people feel confident in their own opinions and conclusions?

Task 3 — Listen to the passage and fill in the blanks with the information you get.

Situation: Here is a passage about communication competence.

Competent communicators have the knowledge and skills to communicate with others in ways that can keep the (1) <u>emotional tone of interactions</u> positive, supportive and non-threatening. They also keep the content of their communication (2) <u>appropriate for the context</u> in which the communication takes place and can employ strategies to manage conflict during the communication when it occurs.

To become a competent communicator within a cultural group, a person needs first, (3) <u>extensive knowledge of the culture</u>, a detailed understanding of the culture and its (4) <u>values, beliefs and behavioral patterns</u>.

Second, (5) <u>fluency of primary language or languages</u> is indispensable. This means the knowledge and skill that (6) <u>are used appropriately</u> to follow semantic, pragmatic and syntactic rules of the language or languages used by the cultural group.

And third, there's a need of (7) <u>a great deal of interaction</u> with members within the culture. It is through (8) <u>socializing with people within a culture</u> that individuals gain intricate knowledge of a culture, its social norms and its rules for languages.

Words and Expressions

supportive *adj.* giving help, encouragement or sympathy to sb. 给予帮助的

semantic *adj.* connected with the meaning of words and sentences 语义的

pragmatic *adj.* connected with the use of language in particular situations 语用的

syntactic *adj.* connected with the rules of forming sentences in a language 句法的

intricate *adj.* complicated 复杂的

attribute *n.* a quality or feature of sb./sth. 属性

ambiguity *n.* the state of being difficult to understand or explain because of involving many different aspects 模棱两可

Lastly, an additional set of attributes is required for a person to become an excellent communicator. When interacting with individuals from a foreign culture, he or she must have a relatively high (9) tolerance for ambiguity. When interactions include people from two or more different cultures, one needs to be fairly comfortable about communicating with people who may have different ways of interacting and behaving. Further, a person should be able to change his or her behavior to (10) accommodate the cultural expectations of others in different communicative situations.

Scripts

Communication competence is the ability to express one's wants, needs and thoughts to others and ways that help them maintain or improve the current state of their relationships. Competent communicators have the knowledge and skills to communicate with others in ways that can keep the emotional tone of interactions positive, supportive and non-threatening. They also keep the content of their communication appropriate for the context in which the communication takes place and can employ strategies to manage conflict during the communication when it occurs.

To become a competent communicator within a cultural group, a person needs first, extensive knowledge of the culture, a detailed understanding of the culture and its values, beliefs and behavioral patterns.

Second, fluency of primary language or languages is indispensable. This means the knowledge and skill that are used appropriately to follow semantic, pragmatic and syntactic rules of the language or languages used by the cultural group.

And third, there's a need of a great deal of interaction with members within the culture. It is through socializing with people within a culture that individuals gain intricate knowledge of a culture, its social norms and its rules for languages. While a person may be a highly competent communicator in his or her primary culture, it does not necessarily follow that his or her competence will transfer to a different cultural setting.

Lastly, an additional set of attributes is required for a person to become an excellent communicator. When interacting with individuals from a foreign culture, for example, he or she must have a relatively high tolerance for ambiguity. When interactions include people from two or more different cultures, one needs to be fairly comfortable about communicating with people who may have different ways of interacting and behaving. For instance, a person needs to be able to cope with situations where he or she doesn't quite know the rules, may not be fluent in the language being spoken and may not agree with the views of others. Further, a person should be able to change his or her behavior to accommodate the cultural expectations of others in different communicative situations.

Task 4 Listen to the passage and answer the following questions.

Situation: Here is a passage about collaboration.

Question 1 What is collaboration?

Collaboration is the ability to share ideas and thoughts openly alongside another person and to come up with a combined answer and a solution about a particular topic or issue. It is the ability to combine different notions, beliefs and theories into one concrete explanation and a solution that is reflective of the diversity of the group itself.

Question 2 Why is there so much weight placed on collaboration?

Every day we interact with many people who all have different perspectives and standpoints. If we know how to deal with the situation and have the ability to collaborate, join forces and pull resources together, we'll have an easier time listening to the other person, understanding him/her, and integrating the strengths of both to work toward the common goal.

Question 3 What is the significance of collaboration?

Collaboration gives people the ability to view information from many angles, allowing them to see or understand something that was not recognized before. Knowing how to collaborate establishes a foundation for more than just one skill. It plays on skills such as communication, time management, problem solving, resource allocation and many more. The benefits of collaboration are endless.

Words and Expressions

standpoint *n.* an opinion or a way of thinking about ideas or situations 立场；观点

tenuous *adj.* so weak or uncertain that it hardly exists 脆弱的；微弱的

Scripts

Have you ever been in a situation where your views and interpretations of the information are so different from someone else's but you are still required to work alongside that person in a group project or assignment? While people are faced with the same situation on a day-to-day basis where they're required to play well with others, that's when the skill of collaboration comes into play.

So, to begin, let's define what collaboration means in simple terms. Collaboration is the ability to share ideas and thoughts openly alongside another person and to come up with a combined answer and a solution about a particular topic or issue. It is the ability to combine different notions, beliefs and theories into one concrete explanation and a solution that is reflective of the diversity of the group itself.

One of the keys for good, effective collaboration is cooperative learning. It is the ability to work with more than one person toward a desired goal. It is the idea of working together toward something that cannot be achieved on one's own.

Why is there so much weight placed on collaboration? Every day we interact with so many people on so many levels who all have different perspectives and standpoints on so many topics and issues. So, what happens when you are placed in a position with someone of opposing viewpoints? As you know, the situation can get tenuous. If you know how to deal with the situation and have the ability to collaborate, join forces and pull resources together, you'll have an easier time listening to the other person, understanding him/her, and integrating the strengths of both to work toward the common goal.

In a nutshell, the idea behind collaboration is giving people the ability to view information from many angles, allowing them to see or understand something that was not recognized before. Knowing how to collaborate establishes a foundation for more than just one skill. It plays on skills such as communication, time management, problem solving, resource allocation and many more. The benefits of collaboration are endless.

 **Speaking**

Task 1 Are you interested in the 21st century skills mentioned in the Listening Section? Work in groups and discuss the one you think the most important in detail, using some of the expressions listed below in your conversations.

Which of the 21st century skills do you think is the most important and why?	Of the 21st century skills, … is really important because … Among the 21st century skills, … is the most important for … As far as I am concerned, the skill of … is a necessity for us to …
What is this skill mainly about?	It is all about … It involves (doing) … It means (doing) …
What benefits do you get from this skill?	The idea behind it is giving me the ability to … If you know how to deal with …, you'll have … By acquiring this skill, you'll find you're becoming …

Task 2 Prepare a two-minute talk about 21st century skills, describing their types, significance as well as the influence on your life.

New skills

▶ ## Communication Skills

Learn to Talk About 21st Century Skills

There are various ways to talk about 21st century skills. One of them may include the following steps:

1. **Begin with the classification of 21st century skills.**

   - 21st century skills include ...
   - 21st century skills refer to ...
   - 21st century skills can be grouped into ...

2. **Describe the significance of 21st century skills.**

   - Learning these skills can help ...
   - The nurturing of 21st century skills is ...
   - 21st century skills can be a good perception to ...

3. **Specify how to acquire 21st century skills.**

   - We should conduct ... in order to ...
   - We should attach importance to ...
   - We should pay special attention to ...

Consolidating: Give a Talk About 21st Century Skills/Competencies

Teaching Tips

1. Familiarize students with the purpose of this section—practicing the communication skills.
2. Call students' attention to the expressions denoting the outline of the talk about 21st century skills/competencies.
3. Have students work in groups of four, make a 5-minute video to talk about 21st century skills/competencies (one student working as the photographer and the other three as participants taking turns talking about 21st century skills/competencies) and then upload the video onto the online learning platform for class sharing and constructive feedback.

Listen to the passage, fill in the blanks with the information you get, and then use them as the outline to make a video to introduce the global practice of developing 21st century skills/competencies.

I. **Classification of 21st Century Skills/Competencies**

1. High-income economies pay special attention to competencies like (1) creativity and problem solving, cross-cultural competence, as well as (2) self-perception and self-control;

2. Middle-income economies emphasize more on competencies like (3) science and technology, art, (4) learning skills and lifelong learning;

3. The findings, based on the research of education policy papers released by (5) 24 economies across the world during the past one and a half decades, abstract a total of (6) 18 competencies.

II. **Significance of 21st Century Skills/Competencies**

1. The nurturing of 21st century competencies is a new direction of (7) education reform worldwide;

2. To better prepare the next generation, 21st century competencies can be a good perception to (8) teach them knowledge and tap their potential;

3. Most of the 24 economies (9) <u>acknowledge the significance of competencies</u> like language, mathematics, humanities, sports and health, critical thinking, communication and collaboration, civic responsibilities and social participation.

III. Acquirement of 21st Century Skills/Competencies

Conducting student-centered, cross-disciplinary and (10) <u>practice-focused learning</u> will be effective in nurturing 21st century competencies.

Scripts

A report has found that high-income economies and their middle-income counterparts are attaching importance to different competencies that their citizens need to have in the 21st century.

High-income economies pay special attention to competencies like creativity and problem solving, cross-cultural competence, as well as self-perception and self-control. In contrast, middle-income economies emphasize more on competencies like science and technology, art, learning skills and lifelong learning, according to *Education for the Future: The Global Experience of Developing 21 Century Skills and Competencies*.

The report was jointly released by China Education Innovation Institute of Beijing Normal University and the World Innovation Summit for Education (WISE) in Beijing. The findings were based on the research of education policy papers released by 24 economies across the world during the past one and a half decades, abstracting a total of 18 competencies.

These economies included China, the United States, Canada, the United Kingdom, France, Finland, Russia, Australia, New Zealand, Brazil, Thailand, Korea, Japan, India, Singapore, Philippines, Malaysia, Indonesia, Qatar, etc.

The research was conducted against a backdrop that many countries and international organizations are thinking about how to nurture their future citizens, to help them better adapt to work and life in the 21st century.

The concept of 21st century competencies was raised as the report was formed under such circumstances, in hopes of providing policymakers, education leaders and researchers with a comprehensive understanding of competencies needed in the 21st century across the world.

"It offers advice on how to nurture these competencies among young people," said Professor Liu, Director of China Education Innovation Institute of Beijing Normal University. He said the nurturing of 21st century competencies is a new direction of education reform worldwide.

"Conducting student-centered, cross-disciplinary and practice-focused learning will be effective in nurturing 21st century competencies," Liu said, adding "it is also emphasized in China's curriculum reform of the 21st century".

The world is changing fast with technological innovation and frequent communication among people from different countries. To better prepare the next generation, 21st century competencies can be a good perception to teach them knowledge and tap their potential.

The report also found that regardless of the income level, most of the 24 economies acknowledge the significance of competencies like language, mathematics, humanities, sports and health, critical thinking, communication and collaboration, civic responsibilities and social participation. However, some competencies, like financial competence, life planning and leadership, have only caught the attention of people in high-income economies.

Practice

Work in groups to make a video about 21st century skills by using the communication skills you have learned in this unit and the outline of the above passage. You can also use some of the expressions in the sections of Listening and Watching which may help make your introduction both informative and interesting. Then upload the video onto the online learning platform for class sharing and constructive feedback.

Goal Checking: Reflect and Evaluate

Work in groups. Reflect on and evaluate what you have learned in this unit, following the directions below.

1. Watch the videos of talking about 21st century skills made by other groups and evaluate them according to the rubric given below.

> **The video is excellent because ...**
>
> - It describes 21st century skills in a detailed manner.
>
> - The use of expressions is idiomatic and the sentences are fluent and cohesive.
>
> - It is well designed, clearly organized and vivid in presentation.

2. Select the best video conforming to the rubric above, watch it again and write down as many words and expressions of 21st century skills as you can to vote for the best presenter.

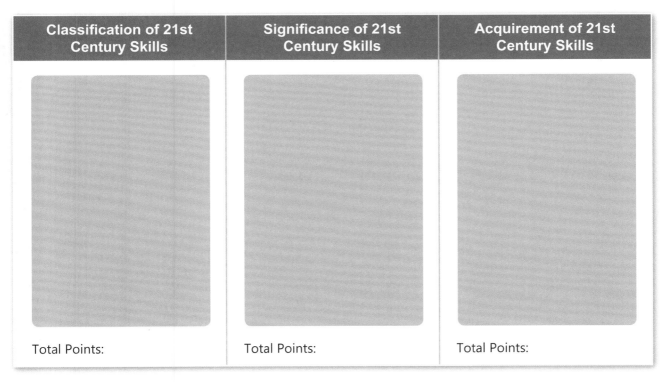

Classification of 21st Century Skills	Significance of 21st Century Skills	Acquirement of 21st Century Skills
Total Points:	Total Points:	Total Points:

Unit 8
Career

■ **Warming Up:** Think and Discuss
Career Paths

■ **Watching and Speaking:** Career Building
Objective: Identify and describe career paths and career building

■ **Listening and Speaking:** Career Choice
Objective: Identify and describe career choice

■ **Consolidating:** Give a Talk About How to Choose a Fulfilling Career
Objective: Talk about choosing a fulfilling career

■ **Goal Checking:** Reflect and Evaluate

CAREER

Unit

8

Warming Up: Think and Discuss Career Paths

Before you start this unit, finish the following exercises with a partner.

1. Listen to the news and discuss with a partner why social enterprise work is a fulfilling career option for many young people.

Keys

Social enterprise work is a fulfilling career option for many people as it brings passion, expertise and social needs together.

2. How many career paths are you considering and which career path do you want to take? Do some research and share what you have found with your partner.

Words and Expressions

come to the fore   to appear 出现

righteousness *n.* the quality of behaving in a way that is morally good 公正

aspiration *n.* a strong desire to have or do sth. 抱负

trial and error   method of solving a problem by making tests until error is eliminated 反复试验法

asset *n.* a useful or valuable quality 财富

CAREER

In recent years, a new form of organization has come to the fore—social enterprises that use commercial means to solve social problems to achieve both "righteousness and profit" and to bring together business purposes and public welfare.

The risk of failure in starting a business is often too high, but statistics show that social enterprises are several times more likely to succeed than other companies. Although social enterprises are privately owned, they have a certain public profile and are therefore more likely to be supported by the community. Social enterprise work is a fulfilling career option for many people as it brings passion, expertise and social needs together.

Young people of this generation are more likely to choose a career that meets their aspirations. They are more likely to have access to social resources and have less time cost and more room for trial and error. And they are more likely to improve their skills in the process of developing social enterprises.

First of all, no absolute failure can be linked with youth entrepreneurship. Social enterprises are never about winning or losing, and the experience of entrepreneurship is a valuable asset for youngsters.

Moreover, in the future, more entrepreneurial opportunities will come from social innovation, and society needs more social enterprises that use market-based solutions to solve problems that may be ignored by regular businesses. And youth development and social enterprises can go hand in hand.

Watching and Speaking: Career Building

▶ Watching

> **Teaching Tips**
>
> 1. Familiarize students with the purpose of this section—identifying career building.
> 2. Call students' attention to Words and Expressions before watching.
> 3. Have students pay attention to the situation of each task.
> 4. Have students do the tasks and check the answers.

Task 1 A Watch the video clip and decide whether each statement is T (true) or F (false).

Situation: Lizzy and Mikel are having a conversation about career building.

(T) **1.** Mikel got bored with his work at the high-tech company.

(T) **2.** Mikel thinks his life is rich in terms of material comforts.

(F) **3.** Mikel dreams of one day becoming a millionaire or billionaire.

(T) **4.** Mikel wants to start his business in ecological agriculture.

(F) **5.** Mikel's parents are crazy about Chinese culture.

Words and Expressions

obsess *v.* to be preoccupied with 迷恋

billionaire *n.* a person who has a billion pounds, dollars, etc. 亿万富翁

rival *n.* competitor 竞争者

tremendous *adj.* very great 巨大的

Scripts

Lizzy: Honey! What's the matter? You look depressed these days. Is there anything wrong?

Mikel: Nothing.

Lizzy: Really? Please, Honey! Please tell me.

Mikel: All right. I quit my job.

Lizzy: What? Your job at the high-tech company?

Mikel: Yes, I quit it.

Lizzy: Why?

Mikel: I can't see any sense in it. I'm dealing with money every moment of every day. But money work can't actually enrich my life, although my life is rich in terms of material comforts. You know, I'm not obsessed with bucks.

Lizzy: Of course, I know you don't care all that much about money.

Mikel: And I don't dream of one day becoming a millionaire or billionaire.

Lizzy: I thought you've been doing really well at the company, getting glowing reviews every year and double-digit salary increase, plus big bonuses at the end of the year too. You must have enjoyed working there, I suppose.

Mikel: For the first couple of years, perhaps. However, I don't feel the thrill of working there anymore. Every day has been such a boring drag lately. I'll take another path. I want to start my business in ecological agriculture.

Lizzy: But in California, and even the US as a whole, the field of eco-agriculture has been overcrowded with rivals, and then you'll have to play the toughest game.

Mikel: I know. I've done some homework and looked into this. Right now, China is witnessing tremendous changes, especially in its west. I'd like to go there and see what I can do.

Lizzy: Wow! I have no idea you have been thinking of such a big move! Sounds exciting!

Mikel: But if we go to China, we'll have to give up the life we've built and enjoyed in this country and try to build a new one in China. That won't be easy, at least in the beginning. Besides, you'll be far away from your parents.

Lizzy: That's true. However, a new life in China sounds like such an exciting prospect, now that I think about it. As to my parents and yours, we can always stay in touch via video calls. Oh, in a year or two, when we've settled down, we can invite them over to see China for themselves. You know my parents are crazy about Chinese culture. They'll be thrilled to know that we're making this big move. Well, honey, I'm all in!

Mikel: I wasn't 100% sure how you'd like this idea. Now I'm all in too!

Task ① B Watch the video clip again and answer the following questions.

Question ❶ Why does Lizzy think Mikel must have enjoyed his previous work?

Because she thinks he has been doing really well at the company, getting glowing reviews every year and double-digit salary increase, plus big bonuses at the end of the year too.

Question ❷ Why does Mikel want to start his career in China?

Because right now, China is witnessing tremendous changes, especially in its west.

Question ❸ How can the couple solve the problem of long distance with their parents if they want to start a career in China?

They can solve the problem by staying in touch via video calls. In a year or two, when they've settled down, they can invite their parents over to see China for themselves.

Task ② A Watch the video clip and fill in the blanks with the information you get.

Situation: Here is a video about how to find talented people.

Brian Acton is (1) an engineering manager who had been rejected by two famous companies before he founded his own company. He thinks (2) the hiring systems built in the 20th century are failing us and causing us to miss out on people with (3) incredible potential. After he (4) consulted with leaders across many sectors, read dozens of reports and research papers, and conducted some talent experiments, he got three ideas:

One: expand our search. One Internet company has built one of the most (5) <u>diverse and high-performing teams</u> to look beyond major tech hubs and focus on (6) <u>designers' portfolios</u>, not their pedigrees.

Two: hire for performance. Brian co-founded a hiring platform where candidates should be asked to (7) <u>demonstrate their skills</u> before they're hired. A candidate should seek out ways to showcase (8) <u>unique skills and abilities</u> outside of just the standard resume and cover letter.

Three: get the bigger picture. As for the employer, it's not correct to have a biased view about someone before he/she knows them well. Only (9) <u>the holistic view</u> of people can help avoid such flawed judgment. We shouldn't (10) <u>equate experience</u> with ability, credentials with competence.

Words and Expressions

quest *n.* a long and difficult search for something 探索

monopoly *n.* the complete control, possession or use of sth. 独占

portfolios *n.* a set of pictures by someone, or photographs of examples of their work, which they use when applying for work （应聘用的）代表作品集

pedigree *n.* background 背景

tryout *n.* a test of the suitability of a performer 选拔

spreadsheet *n.* a computer program used for displaying and dealing with numbers 电子表格

showcase *v.* to display or present to its best advantage 展示

job-hopper *n.* a person who often changes his/her job 跳槽者

holistic *adj.* considering a whole thing 全面的

equate with to consider sth. as being equal to sth. else 认为某事与某事相等

Scripts

We all know people who were ignored or overlooked at first went on to prove their critics wrong. Here's my story. I'm Brian Acton, an engineering manager. I had been rejected by two famous companies before I founded my own company, the mobile messaging platform that would sell for $19 billion.

The hiring systems built in the 20th century are failing us and causing us to miss out on people with incredible potential. So what are the tools and strategies we need to identify tomorrow's high performers? In search for answers, I've consulted with leaders across many sectors, read dozens of reports and research papers, and conducted some of my own talent experiments. My quest is far from over, but here are three ideas.

One: expand our search. If we only look for talent in the same places as we always do, we're going to get the same results we always have. The head of design and research of an Internet company told me that they've built one of the most diverse and high-performing teams in Silicon Valley because they believe that no one type of person holds a monopoly on talent. They've worked hard to look beyond major tech hubs and focus on designers' portfolios, not their pedigrees.

Two: hire for performance. Inspired by my own job experience, I co-founded a hiring platform, which gives candidates an opportunity to shine. Just as teams have tryouts, candidates should be asked to demonstrate their skills before they're hired. If I'm hiring a data analyst, I'll give him/her a spreadsheet of historical data and ask him/her for his/her key insight. And if you're a candidate, don't wait for an employer to ask. Seek out ways to showcase your unique skills and abilities outside of just the standard resume and cover letter.

Three: get the bigger picture. I've heard about recruiters who are quick to label a candidate a job-hopper based on a single short stint on his resume. It's not correct to have a biased view about someone before you know them well. Only the holistic view of people can help avoid such flawed judgment. Let's stop equating experience with ability, credentials with competence.

We could live in a world where people are seen for what they're truly capable of and have the opportunity to realize their full potential. So let's go out and build it.

Task ② B Watch the video clip again and discuss the following questions with a partner.

Question ① How much is Brian's mobile messaging platform worth?

His mobile messaging platform is worth $19 billion.

Question ② If Brian is hiring a data analyst, what test will he give to the candidate?

Brian will give him/her a spreadsheet of historical data and ask him/her for his/her key insight. And he wants the candidate to seek out ways to showcase his/her unique skills and abilities outside of just the standard resume and cover letter.

Question ③ According to Brian, what kind of world could we live in?

We could live in a world where people are seen for what they're truly capable of and have the opportunity to realize their full potential.

▶ Speaking

Task  Work in groups and discuss the pros and cons of the present-day hiring systems in detail, using some of the expressions listed below in your conversations.

What do you think of our present-day hiring systems?	The present-day hiring systems are … They focus on not … but … Under these systems, candidates should be asked to …
How can you get yourselves hired today?	Before we are hired, we should demonstrate … We must seek out ways to showcase our … We must let the employer have the holistic view of …
How do employers hire people?	They do not only look for talent in … They try to give candidates an opportunity to … They try to avoid a biased view about …

Task  Prepare a two-minute talk about your career building, covering all the qualifications you think necessary.

▐▶ Listening Skills

Listen for Cardinal Numbers for Particularizing

When listening for specific information on career, pay attention to the signal words for particularizing. Such signal words as *One*, *Two*, *Three*, *Four*, etc. are cardinal numbers which are often used to specify the steps you must take in order to make your topic statement better understood. For example, if a chef wants to instruct how to cook a delicious dish like sweet sour ribs, he may make his topic statement first and then specify the steps one by one introduced by *One*, *Two*, *Three*, *Four* and *Five* separately. When you listen to this passage, you can take notes of both the topic statement and the cardinal numbers for particularizing with the help of a T-chart drawn as follows.

Topic Statement	Cardinal Numbers for Particularizing
	One:
	Two:
	Three:
	Four:
	Five:

Practice

Listen to the following passage and try to get the topic statement and its cardinal numbers for particularizing by taking notes of them in the T-chart.

Career success typically doesn't happen all on its own and will require effort and determination on your part. If you want to find success with your career, take the following actions.

One: follow your passion. Find success with your career by figuring out what you feel passionate about and making your job go forward.

Two: challenge yourself. It's also important that you continue to challenge and motivate yourself daily so you can grow and develop over the years. Polish and perfect your skills and abilities and be willing to take risks when it comes to your professional life.

Three: be aware of your strengths and weaknesses. The more aware you are of your strengths and weaknesses, the easier it'll be to pick a job that's right for you. You'll find more success with your career when your daily assignments match what you're good at.

Four: set future goals. The only way to truly get ahead with your career is to be diligent about setting goals for what you wish to achieve. You'll be more likely to progress in your current and upcoming roles when you're working toward improving in certain areas.

Topic Statement	Cardinal Numbers for Particularizing
If you want to find success with your career, take the following actions.	One: follow your passion. Two: challenge yourself. Three: be aware of your strengths and weaknesses. Four: set future goals.

Listening and Speaking: Career Choices

▶ Listening

Teaching Tips

1. Familiarize students with the purpose of this section—understanding features and significance of career choices.
2. Call students' attention to Words and Expressions before listening.
3. Have students pay attention to the situation of each task.
4. Have students do the tasks and check the answers.

Task ❶ Listen to the conversation and choose the best answer to each question you hear.

Situation: Li Ming and Chen Min are talking about their career choices.

(C) **1.** What is Li Ming's backup plan?
   A. To get some experience somewhere.
   B. To do interior designing as he's interested in it.
   C. To work in a construction company.
   D. To get into a number of diploma programs.

(A) **2.** What do Chen Min's parents want her to do after college?
   A. To pursue a law enforcement career.
   B. To study in a police academy.
   C. To join the PLA.
   D. To study criminal psychology.

(D) **3.** What does Chen Min decide to do after college?
   A. She's decided to do like her cousin.
   B. She's decided to go home for documents.
   C. She's decided to send applications.
   D. She's decided to be a PLA soldier.

Words and Expressions
backup plan   the second set of plans 后备计划
pan out   to turn out (well or badly) 结果（好或不好）

Scripts

Li Ming: Hey, Chen Min, how are you?

Chen Min: Fine, thanks! Li Ming, I'm thinking about what to do after college.

Li Ming: That's what I've been thinking about too. As you know, I've always been interested in interior designing. That's why I'm trying to get into a couple of diploma programs.

Chen Min: That's great. Have you heard back from any of the programs?

Li Ming: I'll get to know next week.

Chen Min: Do you have a backup plan?

Li Ming: Yeah! My friend's dad runs a construction company. So I'll work there to get some practical experience if my Plan A doesn't work out.

Chen Min: It seems you have everything sorted out.

Li Ming: Well, sort of, and I hope it'll pan out as I've planned. But what do you want to do after college?

Chen Min: Well, I'm in a bind. My parents insist that I should pursue a law enforcement career. That's why I'm studying criminal psychology. But that's not where my heart is.

Li Ming: That's tough. I remember you've told me that your cousin is a senior in a police academy and he has been very helpful, right?

Chen Min: Well, that's true, but I don't want to go that route any more. Some of my classmates have joined the army. I want to be like them, be a PLA soldier to serve the country and grow.

Li Ming: That's a great idea! How did you come up with such an idea? If you have made up your mind, you should send applications now. And you also have to go back home for some documents.

Chen Min: That's what I'm planning to do. I hope my parents will be happy with my choice. After all, studying in a police academy and joining the army are slightly different paths toward the same goals, right?

Li Ming: I wouldn't agree more. Go for it, my friend!

Questions

1. What is Li Ming's backup plan?

2. What do Chen Min's parents want her to do after college?

3. What does Chen Min decide to do after college?

Task ② Listen to the passage and decide T (true) or F (false) before each statement.

Situation: Here is a story about Wu Kaisi's "glittering" career.

(F) 1. With a degree in law and a set of skills, Wu decided to find a nine-to-five office job with a hefty reward package after graduation.

(T) 2. Wu's case highlights the sticky situation of many young Chinese caught between the wishes their parents have for them and their own dreams.

(F) 3. Apart from being a collector of old goods or a hoarder, he has opened up four stores: a coffee shop, a hostel, a designer shop and a bookstore.

(T) 4. Wu is also a photographer, who has traveled around 100 cities, and given more than 20 lectures in various universities across China.

(T) 5. By helping the poor and organizing fundraising events to ask for donations and clothes to the elderly and homeless, Wu has found a sense of happiness that he had never experienced before.

Words and Expressions

hefty *adj.* large 可观的

outdoorsy *adj.* characteristic of or suitable to outdoor life 户外的

flea market an outdoor market that sells secondhand goods at low prices 跳蚤市场

sticky *adj.* difficult or unpleasant 让人为难的

exclusive *adj.* owned by only one person 独享的

fascinate *v.* to attract or interest sb. very much 迷住

discard *v.* to throw sth. away 丢弃

heirloom *n.* a valuable or special possession that has been handed down from one generation to another 传家宝

trinket *n.* cheap showy jewelry or ornament on clothing 便宜首饰

decent *adj.* due 合适的

rebellious *adj.* unwilling to obey rules or accept normal standards of behavior or dress 叛逆的

confront *v.* to face 应对

hoarder *n.* a person who accumulates things and hides them away for future use 囤积者

junk shop a shop that sells cheap secondhand goods 旧货店

thrill *n.* a strong feeling of excitement or pleasure 兴奋感

Wu Kaisi is a fresh graduate with a degree in law and a set of skills which made his friends and family certain that a job with a hefty reward package was just around the corner. But the 22-year-old decided not to pursue a nine-to-five office job, opting for a more "outdoorsy" career which sees him shuttling between flea markets in South China looking for good bargains.

Wu is a "professional" collector of everything old, used and obsolete and the young man could not be any happier. His case highlights the sticky situation of many young Chinese caught between the wishes their parents have for them and their own dreams. "Every single old item is exclusive, and its uniqueness is what truly fascinates me," Wu said, displaying a sense of pride and excitement while talking about his collection.

Born in North China's Shanxi Province and bred in Beijing, his interest in collecting antiques began since childhood years. His parents would take him to Panjiayuan, one of the largest and most popular flea markets in the country, where secondhand goods, discarded family heirlooms and interesting trinkets are a treasure for some.

"My parents used to want me to get a doctoral degree and then find a decent job," Wu said, "but I insisted on keeping my individuality and personality." The independent and rebellious young man spoke about the struggles he went through to confront his family. He described his current job, which has kept him busy for two years, as "garbage picking".

But the young collector has proven his potential in his own way. Apart from being a collector of old goods or a hoarder, he has opened up four stores: a junk shop, a hostel, a designer shop and a bookstore, where he can strategically organize or sell his treasured possessions.

Wu is also a photographer, who has traveled around 100 cities, and given more than 20 lectures in various universities across China, sharing his travels and the countless old and used goods that he collected during his journeys.

It was never Wu's dream to earn a few bucks from selling his collections, but it's his newfound path that led him to a sense of happiness he had never experienced before. The young man has worked to help the poor, organizing several fundraising events to ask for donations and clothes to the elderly and homeless.

Flea markets have given him the excitement and thrill of collecting what he sees as valuable, but sharing these items with others who are in need has offered him another genuine type of joy and satisfaction.

Task ③ Listen to the passage and fill in the blanks with the information you get.

Situation: Here is a talk about SMART goal method for developing a career plan.

(1) Developing a career plan can help you outline a clear path as you begin looking for a job. You'd better write down a series of (2) short and long term goals that will help you achieve your dreams. These goals should not only be (3) relevant to your career at hand and obtainable, but also be tangible so you can measure your progress along the way. Try using the (4) SMART goal method to help you create realistic and attainable career goals as SMART goals are specific, measurable, attainable, relevant and (5) time bound.

Being specific means thinking about what areas you want to improve in and write goals that (6) cater to those areas. Being measurable refers to keeping in mind how much you (7) want to accomplish and how you will know when you've reached your goal. (8) Attainable goals are neither a piece of cake nor impossible mission. Being a millionaire overnight is just a daydream, but you can start to earn and save money day by day to (9) get your start-up capital. Make sure that your goals are really relevant with your career and really matter. Remember to (10) set clear time frames for your goals because without a deadline, you'll have no urgency or motivation to complete your goal.

Words and Expressions

at hand   under consideration 在考虑中的
tangible *adj.* clear enough or definite enough to be easily seen, felt or noticed 清晰可见的
cater to   to provide what is needed to fulfill 迎合

Scripts

Developing a career plan can help you outline a clear path as you begin looking for a job. While it's important to set meaningful career goals, you might become discouraged if these goals are too difficult to achieve. So you'd better write down a series of short and long term goals that will help you achieve your dreams. These goals should be relevant to your career at hand and obtainable. They should also be tangible goals so you can measure your progress along the way. Try using the SMART goal method to help you create realistic and attainable career goals. SMART goals are specific, measurable, attainable, relevant and time bound.

It will be much easier to reach a specific goal rather than a general goal. For example, "Be a better teacher" is somewhat vague. To make it a SMART goal, think about what areas you want to improve in and write goals that cater to those areas. For example, you could say, "I would like to improve the sense of support in my classroom by fostering more one-on-one time with the students." This is a specific goal that's relevant to your career.

The goals you set should be measurable. Ask yourself how much you want to accomplish and how you will know when you've reached your goal. For example, you could say, "I want to increase my sales figures by 20% this year." This will be a measurable goal you will be able to achieve.

Your goals should also be attainable. While you shouldn't make your goals too easy, you also don't want to make them too difficult for yourself. For example, being a millionaire overnight is just a daydream, but you can start to earn and save money day by day to get your start-up capital.

Make sure that your goals are really relevant with your career and really matter. You shouldn't spend time on goals that aren't important.

Remember to set clear time frames for your goals. For example, you could say, "I want to find a job within three months." Without a deadline, you'll have no urgency or motivation to complete your goal.

With the help of the SMART goal method, you'll start your career confidently.

Task ❹ Listen to the passage and discuss the following questions with a partner.

Situation: Here is a talk about how to find career happiness.

Question ❶ Where does the speaker think career satisfaction comes from?

According to the speaker, career satisfaction doesn't come from what we do but from who we get to be while we're doing that job, that is, who our job allows us to be.

Question ❷ What metaphor does the speaker use to explain career satisfaction?

The speaker uses the egg to explain where career satisfaction comes from. The shell is what we do, but the yolk is who we get to be. It is from the yolk where our job happiness comes.

Question ❸ What does the speaker think of her career satisfaction and what can you get from her speech?

It takes a considerable period of time for the speaker to understand where her career satisfaction comes from. When she was young, she thought her career satisfaction came from what she did. As she grows older, she begins to understand that her career satisfaction doesn't come from what she does, but from who she gets to be while doing it.

Words and Expressions

engage *v.* to employ sb. to do a particular job 雇用

credentials *n.* certificates 证书

hummingbird *n.* a small brightly colored bird found in America 蜂鸟

ostrich *n.* a very large African bird with a long neck and long legs 鸵鸟

yolk *n.* the round yellow part in the middle of an egg 蛋黄

perk *n.* sth. you receive as well as your wages for doing a particular job（工资之外的）津贴

wait on tables to work as a waiter 当服务员

despondent *adj.* depressed 沮丧的

epiphany *n.* a moment of sudden insight or understanding 顿悟

Scripts

Research shows that to be happy at work, people want to be engaged. They want to have control over their subject matter. They do want to know that what they do matters more than the paycheck they get.

Why 50% of us can't figure out what we want to do with our life? I think it's because when we're in doubt, we look to our resumes, we look to our credentials and what we're qualified to do. But what we're qualified to do is not necessarily what we're meant to do. And it isn't necessarily what's going to bring us satisfaction.

Think of an egg, if you will. From a little hummingbird egg to an ostrich egg, all of them are roundish shells. For people, that shell is our credentials, our track record, our accomplishments and our resume. A lot of us get attached to that shell. It becomes our identity, and that's what makes it hard to change.

To get to the good stuff, we have to crack the egg open because inside is the yolk. That's where the DNA is. That's what determines how each egg is unique. I call that yolk our "life blueprint". So everything that can be taken away is the shell, the status, our identity, what people think of us, the perks, the salary, but what can't be taken away is the yolk. And that's where the discovery of career satisfaction can happen. Maybe it's more important to understand that career satisfaction doesn't come from what we do. It comes from who we get to be while we're doing that job, that is, who our job allows us to be. That's where the happiness comes from.

So the shell is what we do, but the yolk is who we get to be. When I was in my 20s, I wanted nothing more than becoming a Broadway star. Well, I did reasonably well and I gave myself 5 years to make it. Later, I was still waiting on tables. And so I grew despondent. Why hadn't this dream come true for me? I worked so hard. I invested so much toward that dream for almost 10 years.

Later, I had an epiphany about this, and this epiphany was a spiritual flash that changed the way I viewed acting. The performer was the shell, and causing change from the stage was the yolk. That was me. So I hadn't failed at my dream after all. I just suffered from a misinterpretation of my dream. I needed to allow the dream to change form. I think that's what's wrong for a lot of us when we can't figure it out. That is, no one's taught us to pull the dream apart and understand the true significance of it. And the cure for this epidemic is understanding that career satisfaction doesn't come from what we do. It comes from who we get to be while we're doing it. And the beauty is who we get to be and is the real us.

⫸ Speaking

Task  Are you interested in the career paths mentioned in the Listening Section? Work in groups and discuss how you understand career satisfaction in detail, using some of the expressions listed below in your conversations.

What career are you interested in?	My heart is in … I want to be/opt for … I've always been interested in …
What do you think of setting career goals?	Setting career goals can help me … These goals should be relevant to … The goals I set should be …
Where does career satisfaction come from?	Career satisfaction comes not from … but from … A better way to understand career satisfaction is … What has offered me the genuine type of joy and satisfaction is …

Task **2** Prepare a two-minute talk about a career you want to choose, describing its requirements as well as your reasons for choosing it.

▶ Communication Skills

Learn to Talk About How to Choose Your Career

There are various ways to introduce your career choice. One of them may include the following steps:

1. **Begin with the difficulty of career choice.**

   - It's not very easy to choose ...
   - It can be extremely hard for an adult to ...
   - Choosing the right career is not ... but ...

2. **Evaluate the benefits of correct career choice.**

   - We can benefit from ...
   - The right career choice can bring us ...
   - Our aspirations can be met by ...

3. **Describe the specific steps to take in correct career choice.**

   - Here are some tips for us on ...
   - There are steps we have to take such as ...
   - To find an ideal path requires us to ...

Consolidating: Give a Talk About How to Choose a Fulfilling Career

Listen to the passage, fill in the blanks with the information you get, and then use them as the outline to make a video to introduce how to choose a fulfilling career.

I. **Difficulty of Career Choice**

When it's time to make a career choice in (1) <u>your late teens</u> or even adult years, it can be (2) <u>extremely hard</u> to find the answer.

II. **Benefits of Correct Career Choice**

While your passion might not be your forte, it's (3) <u>a good starting point</u> to help you figure out what career you want to pursue.

III. **Steps to Take in Correct Career Choice**

No.1, make a list of (4) <u>your hobbies</u>;

No.2, discover (5) <u>what you're good at</u>;

No.3, identify (6) <u>your personality traits</u>;

No.4, determine (7) <u>what you want out of a career</u>;

No.5, talk to (8) <u>industry experts</u>;

No.6, research (9) <u>the job market</u>;

No.7, discover (10) <u>your core values</u>.

Teaching Tips

1. Familiarize students with the purpose of this section—practicing the communication skills.
2. Call students' attention to the expressions denoting the outline of the talk about career choice.
3. Have students work in groups of four, make a 5-minute video to talk about how to choose a fulfilling career (one student working as the photographer and the other three as participants taking turns talking about fulfilling career choice) and then upload the video onto the online learning platform for class sharing and constructive feedback.

Scripts

When people are little, they are often asked the question, "What do you want to be when you grow up?" And as a child, the answer is usually something like an astronaut or a firefighter. Still, when it's time to make that decision in your late teens or even adult years, it can be extremely hard to find the answer. Well, here are some tips for you on finding a fulfilling career path.

No.1, make a list of your hobbies. The best place to start with is your hobbies. What are you passionate about? What would make you get out of bed on a cold winter morning to go to work? While your passion might not be your forte, it's a good starting point to help you figure out what career you want to pursue.

No.2, discover what you're good at. What you enjoy and what you're good at can be two very different things. For example, you might enjoy dancing, but you're actually really good at organizing. So being an event planner, an office manager, or a personal assistant may be a sensible choice. When you list your hobbies, create a second list of skills that you possess.

No.3, identify your personality traits. In order to find the right career, you need to take a closer look at your personality traits. While you might be a gifted singer, but if you're too anxious to stand on stage in front of people, then you might not succeed in this field. Therefore, it's important to identify and take into consideration your personality traits when it comes to your career path.

No.4, determine what you want out of a career. It's also necessary to identify what it is that you want out of a career. Do you want to receive a high salary, have a respectable job title or simply work for a cause that you care about? By answering the question, you can narrow down what types of rules you'd be interested in working toward and find the path to success.

No.5, talk to industry experts. Once you've narrowed down a handful of careers, talk to industry experts and find out more about the job and industry as a whole. They will offer insight into the day-to-day practices, working hours, progressions and further opportunities which will help you get a clear understanding of that career.

No.6, research the job market. Besides talking to career experts, you should also research the job market and see whether there are opportunities in this field, or whether it's a career that you'll struggle to secure. You also need to determine whether the role you're interested in has the potential for career progression. Otherwise, you will get bored working in the same position for years on end.

No.7, discover your core values. Identify what your core values are and use them to find a career that is fulfilling for you, make a list of qualities that are important to you and identify companies who have the same core beliefs. This will help you narrow down your search and discover industries that you would be a good match for.

Keep these tips in mind. I think it's not that difficult for you to find the right career path.

Practice

Work in groups to make a video about how to choose a fulfilling career by using the communication skills you have learned in this unit and the outline of the above passage. You can also use some of the expressions in the sections of Listening and Watching which may help make your introduction both informative and interesting. Then upload the video onto the online learning platform for class sharing and constructive feedback.

Goal Checking:
Reflect and Evaluate

Work in groups. Reflect on and evaluate what you have learned in this unit, following the directions below.

1. Watch the videos of talking about a fulfilling career choice made by other groups and evaluate them according to the rubric given below.

The video is excellent because ...
● It describes the fulfilling career choice in a detailed manner.
● The use of expressions is idiomatic and the sentences are fluent and cohesive.
● It is well designed, clearly organized and vivid in presentation.

2. Select the best video conforming to the rubric above, watch it again and write down as many words and expressions of the fulfilling career choice as you can to vote for the best presenter.

Difficulty of Career Choice	Benefits of Correct Career Choice	Steps to Take in Correct Career Choice
Total Points:	Total Points:	Total Points: